101 THINGS FOR A BOY
TO MAKE

OAK BOX, DECORATED WITH CHIP CARVING
ENGLISH, 1648

(VICTORIA AND ALBERT MUSEUM)

101 THINGS FOR A BOY TO MAKE

A.C. HORTH

TEMPUS

In a time before television, before computers, before space travel, before even jet engines, a boy's life was much simpler than it is today. Certainly, he was much handier, would be used to working with tools and certainly capable of making his own entertainment. For the boy with time on his hands, there were the delights of collecting cigarette cards, of going to the cinema on a Saturday morning for the matinee performance of Buck Rogers, of camping with friends in a homemade tent, of helping around the house. And for that boy there was A.C. Horth's *101 Things for a Boy to Make*. A classic of its time, this book prepared its readers for entering the real world, where most men still earned a living through a trade. It taught him how to make things, how things worked and how to amuse himself with items found in every household. It was an invaluable reference work for a lad preparing himself for a trade.

Published in an era before Health & Safety was paramount, some of the things written about are irrelevant today, while others would be considered downright dangerous. It is not advised to make white lead paint, for example, and firing wooden bullets from the toy machine gun could be considered dangerous. Perhaps the model steam boiler might blow up. Certainly, the use of asbestos in its construction would not be allowed! By all means try the simpler tasks nowadays, but use some common sense with the slightly more dangerous things to make.

First published 1928; Second edition 1933; This edition 2007

Tempus Publishing Limited
The Mill, Brimscombe Port,
Stroud, Gloucestershire, GL5 2QG
www.tempus-publishing.com

British Library Cataloguing in Publication Data.
A catalogue record for this book is available from the British Library.

ISBN 978 0 7524 4261 7

Typesetting and origination by Tempus Publishing Limited
Printed in Great Britain

PREFACE TO THE SECOND EDITION

THE gratifying success of " 101 Things for a Boy to Make " has provided the Editor with an opportunity of making additions and the inclusion of a frontispiece.

The fascination of making things is a continual pleasure to the active boy, and in this volume will be found suitable occupation for all boys who can use their hands.

To do is to know ! and practical knowledge is always valuable.

A. C. HORTH.

LONDON.
January, 1933.

PREFACE TO THE FIRST EDITION

IN arranging this collection of 101 Things for a Boy to Make, the Editor has made a wide selection in order to give scope for the beginner who possesses just a few tools with only limited opportunities for using them, as well as for the young craftsman who has had some experience and is skilful with his hands.

There are few boys who do not wish to make useful things, or who would not like to be able to do some of the odd jobs to be found in every household. It is for the boys who are handy with tools and are on the look out for suitable occupation, that this book has been compiled.

In the following pages there is something suitable for every boy who likes to use his spare time in taking up a hobby. There are suggestions for the young woodworker and the metalworker ; for the budding engineer and the model maker. There are opportunities for the outdoor worker, in garden appliances and simple concrete work. There is work for the handyman in dealing with everyday repairs or in adjusting the electric bell, battery or fuse. There are useful things that can be made in the home workshop, on the kitchen table, or by the fireside, and others that can be made in preparation for the holidays and the seaside.

Many of the articles have appeared in the " Junior Craftsman " published by the Institute of Handicraft Teachers, at 6, Laurel Terrace, Leeds, and are reproduced by permission.

CONTENTS

FITTING UP A WORKSHOP.

Many readers who have the use of a spare room or a shed will like to know of an easy method of making a strong work bench which will prove not

Fig. 1

too expensive to construct and will appreciate the following directions. The sketch at Fig. 1 shows the bench in position. First of all cut off a 6 ft. length of 2 in. by 2 in. wood A, and halve in two arms B, each 21 in. long as at Fig. 2. Next secure the long length to the wall at a suitable height, using either rawlplugs, or a cold chisel as at Fig. 3, and fill up the hole with wood. The front piece C, is 9 in. by 1 in, and attached to it are two legs, D and E, cut from 9 in. by 2 in. wood

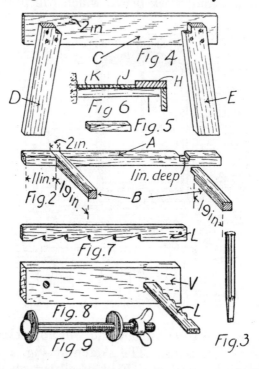

notched to fit against the two arms B. These legs are screwed to blocks, F and G, which are also screwed to the floor and shown at Fig. 5. The top board H, should be 6 ft. by 11 in. by 1½ in., but those behind, at J and K, as shown at Fig. 6, need not be more than ¾ in. thick. The parts of the vice are shown at Figs. 7, 8 and 9 and consist of a length of 9 in. by 1½ in. wood, V, to which a notched arm L as at Fig. 7 is fitted as indicated at Fig. 8. A hole to take the arm is mortised in the leg at E and a hole is bored through the vice leg as well as the front leg to take a 12 in. by ¾ in. bolt as at Fig. 9.

FIG. 10

Those who do not wish to make a bench can easily make an attachment to fit on any strong table, as at Fig. 10. The top piece should be 11 in. wide and the under piece about 9 in. Slots are made to take two G cramps as at A and B. A useful form of bench vice for a table top bench is shown. This can be purchased ready for fixing, but it is not a difficult matter to bore the holes in two pieces of beech and fit two screws which are quite inexpensive to buy. The same kind of bench screw can be fitted to the bench as at

A USEFUL CABINET.

The cabinet shown at Fig. 1 is quite simple in
construction and can be used for a variety of

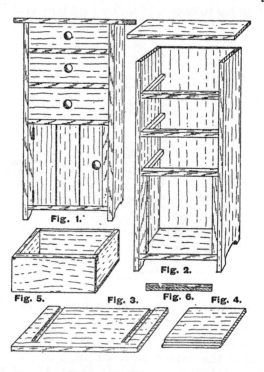

Fig. 1.

Fig. 5.   Fig. 3.   Fig. 6.   Fig. 4.

Fig. 2.

purposes.   A suitable height would be 36 in. with
a width of $16\frac{1}{2}$ in. and a depth of 8 in.   The method
of construction is shown at Fig. 2, the top shown
at Fig. 3 is 18 in. by 9 in. by $\frac{3}{4}$ in. and is stopped
grooved to take the top of the side pieces which are
$35\frac{1}{2}$ in. by 8 in. by $\frac{3}{4}$ in. and rebated along the back
edge as in the section at Fig. 4.   The bottom is

housed in with stopped grooves and the partitions and runners for the drawers, made from 1 in. by $\frac{3}{4}$ in. material, joined at the corners and screwed to the sides. Two strips are placed each side of the door opening and then the drawers and door made. Boxes can be used instead of drawers, but the simple method shown at Fig. 5 will make a much neater job. The door should be made of matchboarding screwed to battens top and bottom as in the section at Fig. 6.

THE CARE AND USE OF WOODWORKING TOOLS.

Woodworking tools do not always get the care they should have ; but if they are treated properly and kept in good condition, it will not be their fault if the work they are called upon to execute is not of the best. There is a good old adage which says, " Bad workmen always blame their tools," and it is as true to-day as it was when some ancient wiseacre first used it.

No self-respecting woodworker allows his tools to be jumbled up together, with the chisels cutting into the sole of the planes and the hammer and pincers destroying the sharp edges of the chisels. It is so easy to obtain a sufficient quantity of wood to make a tool chest and with a packing case and a supply of plywood for making shelves, trays and partitions, there is no reason why tools should not be kept in order.

As a general rule, each tool should be used only for the purpose it is intended ; there is no reason why the chisel should not be used for sharpening a pencil, but the plane should certainly not be used for cleaning off the tops of nails. Timber is a beautiful material to use and its shaping can be made a pleasure and should be a delight; but this can only be when the tools are in good condition. It is often a matter of laziness when woodwork is carelessly done; a cutting tool must be sharp and must be kept sharp and therefore the oilstone should be continually in evidence.

It is essential that the tools should be of the best quality; a chisel that is not made of best cast steel, correctly hardened and tempered, is only a source of trouble. The selection of good tools requires considerable experience, and, as the beginner lacks the essential knowledge, it is really necessary for him to have advice in the purchase of his necessary equipment. There are a large number of tools now on the market which to the inexperienced appear good value, but unfortunately they will not, in a large number of cases, stand the test of wear. Without a considerable amount of knowledge it is almost impossible to judge a tool by its appearance; it is therefore most important that all tools should be purchased from a reputable firm, and above all, they should bear some guarantee.

THE JACK PLANE.

The most useful form of plane for the amateur woodworker is undoubtedly the Jack Plane. It may be used not only for rough planing but if the iron is sharp, it is capable of executing a good finish. Although the wooden plane, shown at Fig. 1, is by far the commoner one, the metal plane has several advantages. No matter how well-chosen and well-seasoned a beech plane is, it is liable to warp and wear, these objections do not apply to the metal plane. The adjustment of the wood plane cannot be so accurately made as in the latter, the main advantage and practically the only one is in the price : a best quality beech

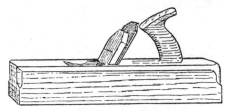

FIG. 1

plane costs 12s. 6d., while a Stanley jack plane costs 21s. This extra cost is worth while as a metal plane will last a lifetime.

The wooden plane should be carefully chosen if a new one is being purchased, the best planes are cut so that the medullary rays of the wood are vertical or at right angles to the sole as shown at A, Fig. 2. This method of cutting out the block minimises the risk of warping. The cutting iron, shown at B, is mainly composed of iron, but a facing of finest steel is welded on as indicated by the lighter portion. This portion of steel occupies less than half the thickness of the blade but is sufficient to provide a keen cutting edge. The cap iron, shown at C, is of steel and slightly curved and is kept close to the cutting iron by means of a screw which fits in the slot of the back iron. The object of the cap iron is shown at D, where the result of the breaking effect of the cap is shown at E. The space between the cutting edge and the edge of the cap iron depends on the wood to be planed. Soft woods such as deal or pine may

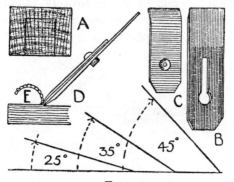

Fig. 2

have a space of $\frac{1}{16}$in., but in the case of hard woods this amount should be reduced to half and even less.

The angle at which the plane iron is fitted in the plane is 45 degrees, the angle of the mitre. The cutting edge should be sharpened on one side only, the correct angle being 35 degrees, while the angle at which the blade should be ground is 25 degrees. These angles are shown at Fig. 2, and should be noted and adhered to in all cases.

HOW TO CUT GROOVES.

Next to the lapped halving joint, the tongue and grove is the simplest form of joint in woodwork. It is almost essential to have a sawing board, this appliance is quite easily made as will be seen in the illustration at Fig. 1. The method of using the board is shown at Fig. 2, the far edge of the board

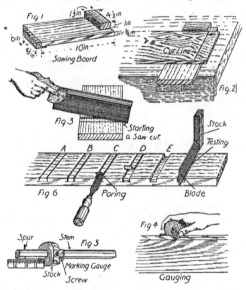

to be cut being pressed up against the end of the sawing board, so that the cut line to be sawn is just outside the projecting piece. All lines to be sawn should be cut in with a marking knife and the saw should be held as at Fig. 3 in beginning the cut. To give the correct depth for the groove, it will be necessary to use a gauge set to the depth as at Fig. 4, the method of setting being shown

B

at Fig. 5, this illustration also gives the names of the various parts of the gauge. The correct sequence of operations in cutting a groove is shown at Fig. 6. A shows the two lines marked out, B shows the same lines sawn, but special attention must be paid to the position of the saw-cut which must be on the waste side of the line and in cutting grooves the waste side is on the inside. The first cut is shown at C and consists in holding a firmer chisel at such an angle that it takes off a wedge-like shaving as at D and when both sides are done in turn, the effect will be similar to that shown at E. The final levelling is done with the chisel held quite horizontal and the test is made with a try-square as shown.

THE MORTISE AND TENON JOINT.

There is very little constructional work in wood that does not contain the mortise and tenon joint, and therefore the craftsman who aspires to good workmanship should be able to make the joint perfectly. It will be seen at Fig. 1 that the end of one piece is cut to form a tenon and is fitted in a hole or mortise cut in another, the two pieces forming a right angle. The joint can be made at an oblique angle as well, but we are not considering that form now.

As a general rule the tenon should be about $\frac{1}{3}$ of the width, but to be accurate, the gauge lines should be set to the width of the chisel nearest in size. The gauge lines should be done if possible with a mortise gauge, but the ordinary gauge as shown at Fig. 2 can be used. The tenon should

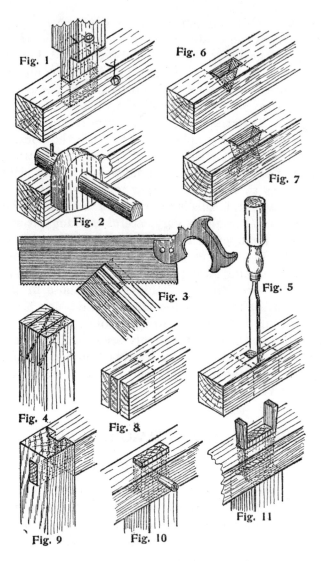

Fig. 1

Fig. 6

Fig. 2

Fig. 7

Fig. 3

Fig. 5

Fig. 4

Fig. 8

Fig. 9

Fig. 10

Fig. 11

be cut with the tenon saw as at Fig. 3, care being taken that the waste of the saw cut is on the waste side of the line. The first cuts are as at Fig. 4, the wood being turned the other way to complete the cuts. In cutting the mortise, hold the chisel as at Fig. 5 and make a V shaped opening as at Fig. 6. Turn the wood over and repeat as at Fig. 7, it will then be a simple matter to finish the sides.

Where the mortise comes at the end of the wood as in the bridle joint, the sides can be cut with a saw as at Fig. 8. Another form of the joint is shown at Fig. 9, this is called the haunched mortise and tenon, it requires very careful marking out and is used for door and similar frames. The pinned joint at Fig. 10 is useful for large joints such as are used in making garden gates, the hole in the tenon is a trifle nearer the shoulder than those in the sides of the mortise, this allows of the tenon being pulled up tight. The wedged joint, Fig. 11, is another method of thoroughly securing the tenon, it is often used in heavy constructional work and in stopped tenons where the tenon does not go through the wood.

USING THE STRAIGHT EDGE.

A Useful Testing Tool.

The straight edge is a testing tool, it is made both in steel and wood, and although the metal tool is more accurate and less liable to damage, it is commonly used by metalworkers. The wooden straight edge is generally found more convenient by woodworkers when testing planed wood. It should be made of a hardwood which is not liable to warp or twist, and as a rule well seasoned mahogany is used. For ordinary purposes a length of beech will be found most suitable, but it must be planed up very accurately with a trying plane. Straight edges vary in length, width and thickness, but a useful size for the woodworker is 30 in. by $1\frac{1}{2}$ in. by $\frac{1}{4}$ in. In use, the straight edge is placed in the direction of the grain of the wood and also from corner to corner as at A and B, and C and D, as shown at Fig. 1. It will be seen that it is a simple matter to test the levelness of the planing in this manner.

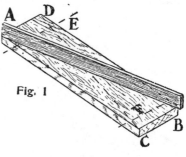

Fig. 1

When the wood to be tested is longer than the straight edge, two straight edges, called winding strips, are placed across the ends of the wood as indicated by the dotted lines at E and F. It is necessary that the two strips should be exactly the same width, and on looking along the top edges of the strips, any deviation from a true level is easily seen. Beginners usually make the mistake of standing too near the first of the two strips, this is a mistake. In order to allow the eye to take in the two strips, it is necessary to stand at least 24 in. away from the first strip, and carefully focus the eye to bring the tops of the strips into line with each other.

The wooden straight edge must be treated with great care. It is usual to hang them up by the side of the bench or against the wall, but the position chosen should be one where they are not likely to be knocked about or bruised by coming into contact with other tools. The careful worker will make a light case from thin ply-wood to hold them, or provide a space in the tool chest or cupboard for them.

MAKING A BOX.

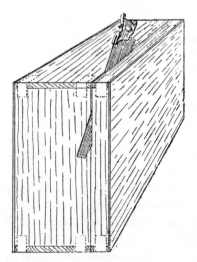

It is not always necessary to use the dovetail joint in box making, the ordinary butt joint, if properly made, nailed together and strengthened with iron angle pieces, will stand a lot of wear.

In making a deal box, of the dimensions say of a length of 2 ft., width 15 in., and height 14 in., the wood for the sides should be ¾ in. thick. Thinner wood is not advisable, but a thickness of ⅝ in. would answer. The ends should be very accurately sawn and should be cleaned up quite square with a finely set plane. The ends of the sides should be allowed to project at least $\frac{1}{8}$ in. and cleaned off after the sides have been nailed to the ends.

The top and bottom should be covered with ply-wood at least $\frac{3}{16}$ in. thick, preferably $\frac{1}{4}$ in., and the angle plates screwed on. The lid portion may then be sawn off as shown. A couple of gauge lines, sufficiently apart to allow for the width of the saw cut, should be made from the top of the box, and the saw carefully guided between the lines. To complete, the sawn edges are planed down to the gauge lines, frequent use being made of the square.

Fillets should be fitted, either inside the lid or on the sides of the bottom portion ; the former method is generally more convenient.

Extra strength can be given by nailing on a plinth formed by 2 in. by $\frac{3}{4}$ in. wood, chamferred on the top edge and mitred at the corners.

THE COMMON DOVETAIL JOINT.

The common dovetail joint as at Fig. 1 is really not difficult at all when it is understood, but its appearance is against it. If the sequence from a plain notch joint is followed, the principal idea may be seen without difficulty. Figs. 2 and 3 illustrate a single notch joint open and closed. This joint may be pulled apart in either direction either by pulling out the part A called the pin, or B termed the socket.

Supposing we were to decrease the width of

the top of the pin or increase the bottom as shown by the dotted lines at Fig. 3, and make the socket hole to correspond, we should have a joint similar to Figs. 4 and 5 which shows it closed and open.

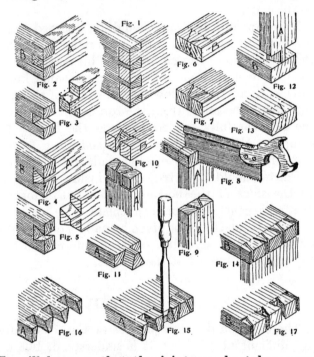

It will be seen that the joint can be taken apart in one direction by withdrawing the pin.

We have now a single dovetail joint. There are two ways in which this joint may be made, and in order to prevent confusion it will be as well to describe the method of procedure with the single joint. First set out the socket on the piece B, as shown at Fig. 6. Next saw down the lines as shown at Fig. 7, and then place the piece on the top of the A piece and mark through with the saw as shown at Fig. 8. The top of A piece when B has been removed will be as shown at Fig. 9, and all we have to do is to saw on the *outside* of the saw marks. It is a help to draw lines down the sides with a square as suggested by the dotted lines at Fig. 9. and then it will be easy to saw the pin. To complete the joint remove the waste in A and B as suggested at Fig. 10 and fit together.

The other method is perhaps easier for the beginner. The pin A is made first, marking and cutting it out as shown at Fig. 11. Saw it down and cut away the waste on each side and then place it on B, which should have a line across equal to thickness of A as shown at Fig. 12. The shape of the end of the pin resting on B should be marked with a pencil or knife point and will appear as shown at Fig. 13. The lines should be squared down the edge and then the saw cuts made on the *inside* of the line as shown at Fig. 7. The waste should be cut away with a chisel as before and the joint fitted.

It should not be a difficult matter now to tackle a similar joint with several pins. The method of marking for the sockets is shown at Fig. 14, both pieces of wood having lines across equal to the thickness. The saw cuts should be made in the pins and they should be cut out in exactly the same way as the single method, with the addition of the waste between the pins, which must be removed with a chisel as suggested at Fig. 15, and when complete will be as shown at Fig. 16. If the pins are made first, the wood should be placed on top and sockets marked as before, the saw cuts being made and waste being removed in the same way ; the method to be followed in cutting the waste of the sockets is shown at Fig. 17.

The principal points to remember are, first mark out accurately, next saw on the waste side of the line ; in the case of pins on the outside of the line and in the sockets on the inside. If these cuts are done properly, the making of the dovetail joint will be easy.

In setting out a dovetail joint it is advisable to have as many pins as possible and have them as fine or thin as can be conveniently made. The amount of bevel shown in the accompanying diagram is much more than is really necessary. The slope should be just sufficient to hold the dovetail together. A good method of judging the number and size of the pins is to examine a well made drawer and work in proportion.

SOME SIMPLE CORNER JOINTS.

The simplest method of joining the ends of two pieces of wood is shown at Fig. 1 and is known as the " butt " joint. The ends of both pieces must be quite square as indicated at Fig. 2, and in sawing and any subsequent cleaning up with the plane or chisel, constant use of the trysquare is essential in making a true joint. The two pieces should be glued and strengthened further with nails or screws.

When additional strength is needed an adaption of the bridle joint is used as indicated at Fig. 3.

In this case we have portions of both ends interlocking. In marking out the two ends as shown at Fig. 4, care must be taken that the marks on each piece correspond. The marks across the grain should indicate exactly the thickness of the wood and the lines along the grain drawn at the same time with a marking gauge, to give accuracy. In sawing out the parts, care must be taken to mark the waste, and saw only on the waste side of the line as shown, in order that each part will fit accurately as shown at Fig. 5.

A development of the above joint is shown at Fig. 6 in the form of the lock-corner joint, a method now commonly utilised by machine box makers. The ends are usually divided into divisions equalling the thickness of the wood, but this is, of course, not essential. Marking out is on the same method as the previous joint and is shown at Fig. 7 ; gauge lines being a necessity if the work is to be done well. The inner corners of the notches must be perfectly clean and quite square as shown at Fig. 8, and although the joint is really quite simple it requires careful work.

Quite another type of joint is shown at Fig. 9, and is very useful when a neater method of applying the butt joint is required. The full width of one piece is fitted in the notched or rebated end of the right angle piece. The amount of material left on the notched end should be sufficient to prevent it splitting off; a rough proportion allows of three quarters of the thickness for the depth of the notch. The method of marking out is to square off a line across the grain equal to the thickness of the wood and then gauge a line on the end grain, as indicated at Fig. 10, to give the depth of the notch. When cut out the joint will appear

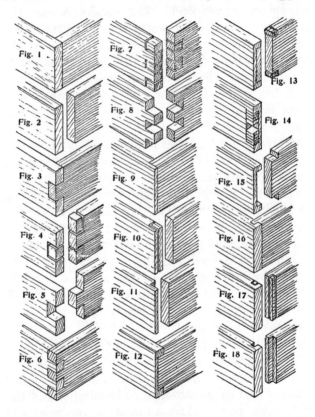

as shown at Fig. 11, and if the saw cuts are quite square and clean it is ready to fit together. Glue and nails or screws may be used, or the inside corner may be strengthened with glued corner blocks if nail holes would be inadvisable.

A combination of this joint with the bridle joint is shown at Fig. 12, it is very similar to the joint at Fig. 3, but the end does not project through the wood. The pieces should be marked out as shown at Fig. 13, gauge lines being used to obtain accuracy. The corners of this joint must be particularly true, but if the centre notch is carefully chiselled out as indicated at Fig. 14, and the end sawn out square as shown at Fig. 15, it should fit quite tightly and give a particularly neat appearance on the end grain.

A description of simple corner joists would not be complete without showing the tongue and groove joint shown at Fig. 16; this is a development of the joint at Fig. 9 and forms a very strong joint particularly in thin wood. The gauge should be used as far as possible in marking out, and in very thin wood the use of the saw may be dispensed with if a sharp gauge is used. The length of the tongue and depth of the groove should as a rule be half the thickness of the wood as shown at Fig. 17. In cutting out, the notched end may be entirely sawn, but the waste of the groove must be removed with a suitable chisel so as to leave clean corners as shown at Fig. 18.

FIRST STEPS IN MAKING WORKING MODELS.

A STEAM TURBINE MOTOR.

Many mechanical working models can be made out of scrap and odds and ends, but not without

care and forethought. The turbine shown in
section, end view and plan at Figs. 1, 2 and 3 can
be made from a large and a small boot polish tin
together with a few scraps of wood and metal.
First clean the two tins and then cut out pieces
of paper to the exact size of the inside of each,
drawing the circles with a pair of compasses.
Place the papers inside the tins and lids and mark

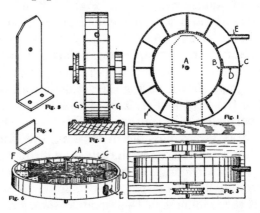

Fig. 5
Fig. 4
Fig. 2
G> <G
Fig. 1
E
A
B
C
D
F
Fig. 3
Fig. 6
F
A
C
D
E

the centre with a centre punch. Next provide
a 4 in. wire nail which will act as a spindle and
find a drill of the same diameter with which to drill
holes. Next fit the spindle and place the smaller
tin inside the larger and measure the distance
between the outer circumference of the smaller
to the inside of the larger. At Fig. 1, A represents
the spindle, B the smaller tin and C the larger.
The blades at D are a little shorter than the dis-
ance between B and C and a little narrower than
the inside of the larger tin when closed. As
many blades as can be conveniently fitted should

be soldered to the inner tin, this being thoroughly cleaned on the edge. The blades should have a flange as at Fig. 4. Allowance must be made for a thin washer on each side of the inner tin and the blades must revolve easily without touching the large tin. Fig. 6 shows the inner tin fitted with blades in position. The next step is to fit a short length of tube about 1 in. long and $\frac{1}{8}$ in. diameter as at E and solder it in. Copper tube can be bought, but a short length can be easily made from a scrap of tinned sheet folded over a wire nail and soldered. A hole about $\frac{3}{16}$ in. diameter is cut out of the larger tin on the edge at F. The outer tin after being sealed with solder round the joint is supported on two uprights as at G, shown separately at Fig. 5, they should be attached with solder and about 1 in. wide. The base can be any convenient size. The two pulleys can be of sheet brass or cast in lead, and soldered to the spindle, wood should be avoided. A diameter of $\frac{3}{4}$ in. to 1 in. will be sufficient.

A MODEL STEAM BOILER.

A boiler suitable for use with this motor is shown at Fig. 1. The upper portion is a lever lid tin similar to those used for golden syrup, the lower tin is of a size that the upper tin will easily fit in. A length of copper or tin tube is soldered to the top of the upper tin, the lever lid acts not only as an opening for filling, but a safety valve. The lower tin is pierced about $\frac{1}{2}$ in. down and the cuts turned inwards to provide projections for the top tin to rest on, as at Fig. 2. A hole is cut to take the lamp, and cuts are made round the base for draught.

The lamp, Fig. 3, is made from a small tin lid bound with wire-twisted to form a handle. Actual

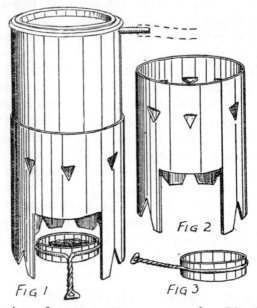

FIG 1   FIG 2   FIG 3

dimensions do not matter very much. The lamp it fitted with shreaded asbestos packing or cotton wool, and filled with methylated spirit.

A MODEL WINCH.

A winch is not difficult to make, one suitable for fitting to a model crane or for innumerable other purposes is shown at Fig. 1, and the various parts are indicated at Fig. 2. A represents the upright supports, B the base, C is the drum on which the rope is wound and un-wound, D the flanges at the end of the drum, E is a large cogged wheel attached to the spindle of the drum and F is the handled crank. A small cogged wheel G is fixed to the crank and engaged with the large

FIG 1

cogged wheel E, so that in turning the handles the drum is revolved. The pawl H is arranged to fit in teeth of a notched wheel at J, so that the handle can be secured at any position.

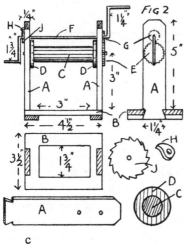

FIG 2

The wood used for the framework should be $\frac{1}{4}$ in. thick and the drum worked to a diameter of 1 in. The cog wheels can be made from sheet brass, but wheels from an old alarm clock can be adapted.

HOW TO MAKE MODEL AEROPLANE PROPELLERS.

There are several methods of making model propellers for aeroplanes, the easiest and quickest

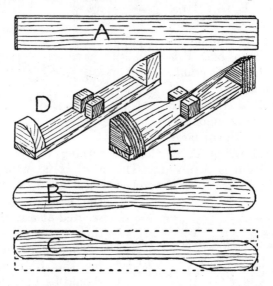

is to use thin wood, veneer is quite suitable, and shape it from a piece as at A, to the shape at B or C. If veneer is used, it can be cut and shaped with a sharp knife and it is better to use a close-grained hardwood. The piece of wood should be steamed or placed in boiling water for some minutes and then fixed in a frame as shown at D. This frame should be made to suit the length of the propeller and should be about the same width as the blade. The blocks at the end should be nearly right angle triangles with a curve as shown. The steamed wood is placed in the centre slot and then the blades tied to the two curved blocks at the ends, and left until quite dry. The wood always springs

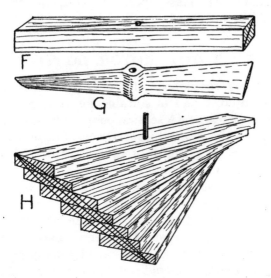

back a little, so due allowance must be made if a course pitch is desired.

The propeller should be smoothed with glasspaper and polished; the smoother the surface obtained the better.

Another method of making a propeller is to curve it out of a block of wood as at F. The centre hole should be bored and a diagonal marked on the ends in opposite directions. With the aid of a pocket knife, a rasp, file and then glasspaper it is possible to make a propeller of the shape shown at G. The built-up propeller at H is made of a number of strips of thin wood, strung on a length of wire and glued together. When the glue has set, the ends can be marked out as shown and the edges cut away with chisel, rasp, and file and finished with glasspaper. A built-up propeller should be varnished or polished.

A TOY MOTOR BOAT.

The toy speed boat at Fig. 1 will be found of great interest and is suitable for use on a small pond, a stream or a seaside pool. The dimensions are not of the greatest importance, but a convenient size would be a length of 10 in., a width of $2\frac{1}{2}$ in., and a depth of $1\frac{3}{4}$ in.

It will be seen that the motive power is derived from two lengths of twisted rubber attached to propellers, and providing that the weight of the rubber does not amount to more than the wood can support, there is no reason why many different sizes and shapes should not be experimented with. The formation of the hull should not cause much trouble, the top is recessed as shown at Fig. 2, a saw cut is made in the centre and the sloping portion of the hull can be cut out with chisel or saw.

The support for the propellers can be made of brass wire about $\frac{1}{8}$ in. diameter, but to allow for the strain of the twisted rubber, the sides of the supports should be flattened out with a hammer on a flat piece of iron. The same applies to the front supports or hooks for the rubber as shown at Fig. 4. If the wire were left round, the strain of the rubber when fully twisted, would soon pull the hooks out of shape. The propellers are made of either tinned sheet or sheet brass, the latter material is much more satisfactory. The hooks should be stiffened by hammering on the sides

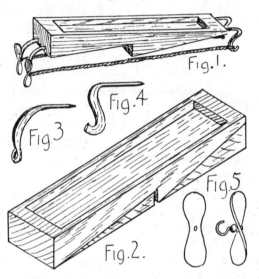

Fig. 1.

Fig. 4

Fig. 3

Fig. 5

Fig. 2.

and they should be fitted with small glass beads to act as bearings.

An alternate method of making a motor boat of similar shape is to build it up with thin wood and arrange the rubber strands inside the boat.

MOUNTING HOMEMADE COILS.

The illustrations at Figs. 1 and 4 give two methods of mounting coils which are quite as satisfactory in use as those sold for the purpose in the shops. The simple mount at Fig. 1 is suitable for single

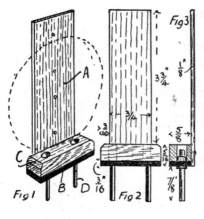

wound basket coils. The back, A, should be $\frac{1}{8}$ in. hardwood, the block, B, of vulcanite and the top of the block, C, of any wood. The pins, D, are screwed to the vulcanite block and fit into ordinary valve sockets. Connections from the coil are made to the top of the pins through the holes in the piece C.

The larger mount at Fig. 4 is made with a vulcanite base, A, Fig. 6, about $1\frac{1}{4}$ in. by $\frac{1}{2}$ in. or so, depending on the thickness of the coil. A suitable strip of cardboard, B, passes round the outside of the coil and is fastened to the shaped block, C, Fig. 5, which is screwed to the vulcanite mount. Holes are drilled through the block, C, to take the two pins as in the section at Fig. 7.

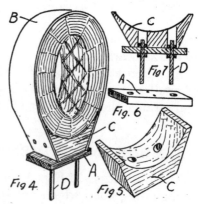

A WINDMILL

An easily made windmill is shown in front elevation and side section at Figs. 1 and 2, and in the latter illustration it will be seen that the sails are attached to a boss joined to a spindle, and turn a pulley which is attached by a belt to another pulley, working on a spindle, to the outside of which is attached a third pulley. The front and back pieces of the house portion are made to the same size as shown at A in the diagram at Fig. 3. The wood should be 12 in. by 7 in. by $\frac{1}{4}$ in. when finished. In marking the pieces out, a centre line should be drawn from top to bottom and a line drawn across 2 in. from the top. A distance of $2\frac{3}{4}$ in. should be marked on this line from the centre, and from the outside points, lines can be drawn to the top to give the correct slope of the roof. The waste wood should be sawn off and planed down smooth, taking care to keep the edges square. The side pieces are shown at B and are finished to 10 in. by $4\frac{1}{4}$ in. by $\frac{1}{4}$ in. These four pieces should be placed together so that the correct slope on the top edges of the sides can be marked out and planed down so that the roof pieces will fit flat. The two pieces for the roof are cut to $5\frac{3}{4}$ in. by 5 in by $\frac{1}{4}$ in. as at C, the front, back and bottom edges are quite square, but the top edge of each piece is planed to a slope so the apex will meet when the pieces are in position. The base of the model is made with $\frac{1}{2}$ in. wood so as to give solidity to the construction, four pieces of wood are required, one is 9 in. by 7 in., this forms the base proper as at Fig. 4. On top of this piece is glued another piece 6½ in. by 4¼ in. by ½ in., but the ends are planed to the same slope as the sides as at **D**, thus making the length measured on the top to 6 7⁄16 in. or perhaps a little

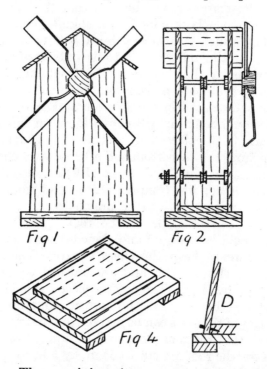

Fig 1

Fig 2

Fig 4

D

less.   The remaining pieces are 7 in. by 2 in. by ½ in. and they are glued to the under side of the larger piece as shown at Fig. 4.   The various fittings for the sails and pulleys should now be prepared, and first of all two lengths of birch dowel rod ⅜ in. diameter should be provided for the spindles. One length for the top should be 6½ in. long as at

E, the other length being 6 in. The boss, F, to
fit on the top spindle, and to which the sails are
attached, is $2\frac{1}{8}$ in. diameter and $\frac{5}{8}$ in. thick. It
be should made from a piece of close grained wood
such as sycamore or birch by marking the diameter

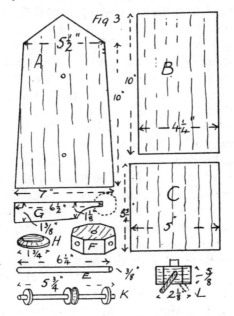

Fig 3

on a block of the required thickness and first
drilling a hole to provide a tight fit for the spindle;
this should be carefully attended to. The shape
can be pared with a sharp chisel. The four sails
are cut from $\frac{3}{16}$ in. wood to a length of $6\frac{1}{2}$ in. and
an end width of $1\frac{3}{8}$ in., as at G. The slope is
marked off 4 in. from the end to a width of $1\frac{1}{8}$ in.
and from this point the wood is scooped out to
give an end $\frac{1}{4}$ in. wide, this can be done with a

sharp knife. Four holes should now be drilled
in the circumference of the boss, they should be
equally spaced and drilled to a depth of $\frac{3}{4}$ in. with
a $\frac{3}{16}$ in. bit and arranged in the centre of the thickness. The pulley wheels and bosses are cut from
$\frac{3}{16}$ in. wood to a diameter of $1\frac{1}{4}$ in. and drilled with
the centre hole of $\frac{3}{8}$ in. diameter, those forming
the pulley wheels as at H should be chamfered
on the inner edges so as to form a V-shaped groove
when the two pieces are glued together. The holes
in the plain pieces should be a fairly slack fit, but
those in the pulley pieces should be a good fit so
that the wood will fit quite tight. The pieces
are arranged on the spindle as at K, but before
this can be done the holes in the front and back
pieces must be drilled. The position of the holes
is shown at A, Fig. 3, the top one is 4 in. down and
the second is 6 in. below. In the latter case the
hole in the front piece should not be carried right
through the wood but should enter a little way
from the back to give the correct position. The
plain wheels should be so placed on the spindles
that they are exactly $4\frac{1}{2}$ in. from outside to outside,
and the pulley wheels exactly in the centre between
them; the top spindle projects 1 in. in front and
$\frac{1}{2}$ in. at the back, and at the bottom the projection
is 1 in. at the back. The front and back pieces
can now be nailed or screwed together with the
spindles in position and the plain pieces at the
ends touched with a little blacklead to enable
them to move easily. The upper part can now
be screwed to the base and then the bottom pulley
and the top boss glued on the ends of their res-

pective spindles. The sails are now fitted in position, but this can be done before the boss is glued on if desirable, the position of the slope of the sails is shown in the plan at L, each sail being fixed at the same slope. The belt connecting the two inner pulleys is made with string and tied fairly tight. The windmill should now be tested and if correct adjusted, the top pieces forming the roof can be bradded on. A coat or two of paint or varnish will add to the appearance of the finished model.

A SPRING-OPERATED TOY MACHINE GUN.

A machine gun, firing wooden ammunition as fast as the crank can be turned, as shown in the accompanying illustration, can be made very easily. The wooden gun barrel is turned down to 7 in. by 1 in., tapering to $\frac{5}{8}$ in., and bored $\frac{1}{4}$ in. diameter. A slot is cut near one end, reaching down to the bore, to allow the ammunition to drop from the magazine into the barrel. The underside of the barrel is rounded off, as shown, for the spring which must pass under from the rear. The barrel is then mounted between two wooden supports attached to a base. A piece of stiff clock spring is fastened securely into a slot cut in the shaft, which is a round piece of hard wood. It is fastened by riveting a small brad through the wood and through a small hole punched in the spring. The shaft is mounted just below the rear end of the gun-barrel, so that the spring will slip against the lower " shell," after first catching on a projection left in the upper part of the barrel. When the crank on the shaft is turned, the spring strikes this projection, bends backwards, then slips forwards with a jerk, which drives the wooden bullet forwards with great force. The shaft is held at exactly the right point to keep the spring in place, by putting a cotter pin in each end of the shaft,

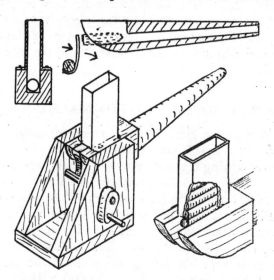

with a washer between each cotter pin and the support, to keep the pin from cutting into the wood. The crank may be either a piece of sheet metal with a small bolt for a handle, or a piece of wood, with a wooden handle. The end of the shaft is cut square so that it will turn with the crank. For a magazine, a piece of tin is bent and soldered into a shallow box, 3 in. by 1¼ in., with open ends. At the lower ends lugs are provided, to keep the magazine in place. The wooden bullets, $1\frac{1}{8}$ in. by $\frac{3}{16}$ in., are slipped into the upper end of the magazine. When the crank is turned, the spring drives the bullets out one by one, a new bullet falling into place as the one before is fired. If well made, this machine gun should work rapidly, and should fire bullets several yards, and with great force.

A VERNIER CONDENSER.

The simple form of condenser apparatus shown in perspective at Fig. 1, and in section at Fig. 2, is connected up in parallel with another condenser for sharp tuning. It is very easily made with a little teak, some tin from an empty tobacco box and a sheet length of screwed rod with nuts.

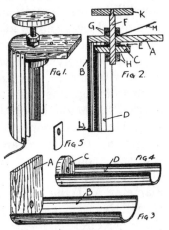

The piece at A is $2\frac{1}{4}$ in. by $1\frac{1}{2}$ in. by $\frac{1}{4}$ in. with the end rounded to a radius of $\frac{3}{4}$ in. The piece at C is 1 in. diameter and $\frac{1}{4}$ in. thick. A centre hole of the same diameter as the screwed rod is bored through each. The plate at B, Fig. 3, is 4 in. long and half the circumference, that at D, Fig. 4, is also half the circumference, but $3\frac{1}{2}$ in. long, but a $\frac{5}{8}$ in. by $\frac{1}{2}$ in. strip at Fig. 5 is soldered on the curved edge, to the top edge of plate D, as at E, Fig. 2, the hole coinciding with that in C. The parts are joined with a short length of screwed rod F, double nuts G are fastened about ½ in. or so down, a washer is inserted between A and the plate E on top of C and double nuts are also fastened at H. The knob can be made of teak about 1¼ in. diameter and the rod filed as shown at K. Connections are made by soldering wire to L and attaching to M.

TWO FLYING TOYS.

There is a peculiar fascination in all kinds of flying toys and these two examples will provide for skill in construction and interest in flying them. The metal flyer shown at Fig. 1 consists of a piece of tinned sheet about 5 in. diameter, about 16 in. of brass or galvanized wire, a cotton reel, some extra wire and an old bradawl handle. The ring shown at Fig. 2 is quite simple, the vanes, shown at Fig. 3, should be of the same diameter as the ring, the actual proportions are not so important as getting the three vanes of the same size and the same inclination. As a guide, the outside of the vanes can be 1½ in., the inner circle ¾ in. diameter and the inner width of the vanes ⅝ in. It will be seen at Fig. 3 that the lines forming the inner circle are carried half way through the smaller ends of the vanes and in cutting out the shape these lines should be cut through.

Three holes are drilled through the centre to fit on the wire. The reel, shown at Fig. 4, should fit easily on the length of wire which is driven into the bradawl handle as at Fig. 5, and two short lengths of wire are driven into the top of the reel to match the holes in the vanes. File a nick in the outer edges of the vanes and fit on the wire ring and solder to complete. A small ring should be

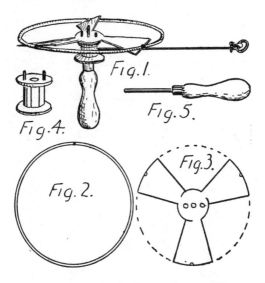

Fig. 1.

Fig. 5.

Fig. 4.

Fig. 2.

Fig. 3.

fastened on the end of the string. The position of the vanes should be altered until the best flying angle is discovered.

The vanes of the wooden flyer at Fig. 6 should be made of hard wood if possible. The two portions are halved together as at Fig. 7 and should be about 8 in. by $1\frac{1}{2}$ in. by $\frac{1}{4}$ in. or $\frac{3}{8}$ in. The ends should be marked with a diagonal line and the waste wood pared off with a chisel or pocket-knife.

The spindle should be of birch dowelling and

fit tightly into the centre of the vanes. The holder can be made from a 6 in. length of 1½ in. wood with the sides shaped to an octagonal form as at Fig. 8, two ¼ in. thick pieces are glued and screwed to opposite sides, the top piece being bored

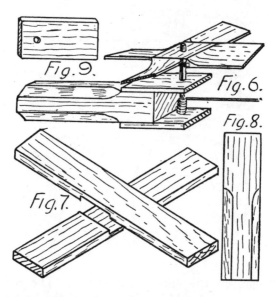

Fig. 9.

Fig. 6.

Fig. 8.

Fig. 7.

to take the spindle as at Fig. 9, and the under piece bored half way through so that the end of the spindle can rest in it while it is being wound up. Fit a ring to the end of the string and rub a little blacklead in the holes to enable the spindle to run easily. In use, the string is wrapped tightly round the spindle and then pulled sharply. The propeller will rise up quickly and mount to a considerable height.

HOW TO MAKE KITES.

There are quite a large number of different kinds and shapes in kites, one of the commonest and easiest to make is the ordinary peg-top pattern shown at Fig. 1. The backbone should be a stiff piece of wood, for a large kite it can be 3 ft. long

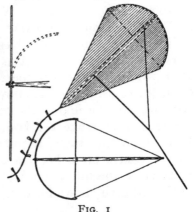

FIG. 1

and about twice as wide as it is thick, the latter dimensions depend on the kind of wood used; with ash, the size can be 1 in. by $\frac{1}{2}$ in. at the thickest part. The bow should be of cane, ordinary rattan or split bamboo, the latter generally being the most serviceable. For a backbone of 3 ft., the length of the cane for the bow should be 33 in. The bow string is tied to the backbone and to the ends of the bow, making a distance between of 21 in. The covering can be thin glazed calico or

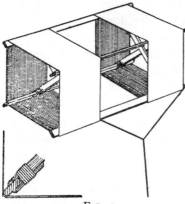

FIG. 2

aeroplane silk, the sides are sewn or pasted to strings fastened to the ends of the bow and the bottom of the backbone. The box kite shown at Fig. 2 is formed with four 30 in. lengths, each $\frac{7}{16}$ in. by $\frac{3}{16}$ in. with outer edges rounded. The cross bars are $\frac{1}{2}$ in. by $\frac{1}{4}$ in. The material is cut to 10 in. wide and each of the four sides are 15 in. long, the edges being folded over and pasted down with wire in the fold. The method of fitting the material is to make the two endless bands first, then fit on the frame, adjustments can be made to the centre cross bars in order to stretch the material to the full amount. The correct position of the strings is shown for both kinds of kite.

DRAUGHT AND CHESS BOARDS.

The draught or chessboard shown in the illustration is made with a glass top and the construction is different from the usual form of built up squares of two coloured woods. The actual dimensions depend on individual choice, but a suitable size may be based on squares of $1\frac{1}{4}$ in. With eight squares of $1\frac{1}{4}$ in., the chequer space is 10 in. each side, this with a space of 1 in. for border each side, will bring the exposed glass surface to 12 in. As will be seen in the elevation and section, the glass is enclosed in a frame of ordinary picture moulding; allowance must therefore be made for the amount of the rebate which will probably be $\frac{1}{4}$ in.

First provide a piece of glass, say $12\frac{1}{2}$ in. square, a sheet of hot pressed hand made paper or a sheet of Bristol board of the same size; about 5 ft.

of 1¼ in. plain oak picture moulding and a piece of ply wood a little over 14 in. square.

The paper should be pinned down on a drawing board and ruled out in 1¼ in. squares, using a T square and set square. The black squares are

now filled in with Indian ink, but if there is likely to be any difficulty to obtaining a straight line with a brush, the lines can be drawn with a pen first and the inside filled with ink when dry, the paper should be cleaned up with soft rubber.

The frame is made in the usual way, using an ordinary mitre sawing block. Considerable care should be taken to make the inside of the moulding exactly 12 in. or whatever size is decided on.

HOT-AIR BALLOONS.

Balloons made of tissue paper and inflated by means of hot-air are easily constructed and are very interesting both from the constructional and flying aspects. The first thing to do is to provide

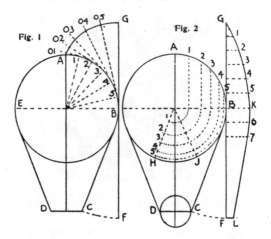

sufficient tissue paper of good quality and then to mark out the shape of the gores.

Taking a diameter of 3 ft. as a useful size, set out the diagram at Fig. 1 with a quadrant AB divided into six parts and the lines O1 to G drawn tangent to the several radii. Mark off lengths A1 on O1, from 2 to O1 on O2, from 3 to O2 on O3 and so on. The total length of the gore is from G to F and the shape of the sides is obtained as at Fig. 2. BG is divided into six parts, two similar spaces being marked below as at 6 and 7. The widths are taken from the triangle, HJ being $\frac{1}{8}$ of the circumference

enclosing 45°. 6 and 7 being equal to 5 and 4.
The bottom is similarly marked off. Make the

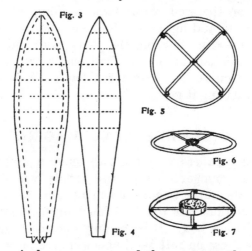

Fig. 3

Fig. 5

Fig. 6

Fig. 4

Fig. 7

pattern in brown paper and then cut out the gores
1 in. wider all round, pasting the tissue sheets together to make up the necessary size. When the
8 gores, Figs. 4 and 5, are ready, and they are
more effective when in different
colours, paste them together,
taking care that the pieces do
not stick together anywhere
but at the seams. Paste a
circular piece on top, and
paste the bottom to a wire
ring as at Fig. 5. Attach
some cotton wool as at Fig. 6,
or a small lid as at Fig. 7 and
then the balloon is ready,
as shown at Fig. 8.

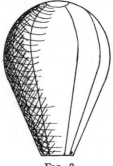

Fig. 8

Choose an evening free from wind, get some help in opening out the sides, pour some methylated spirit on the wad or on some wadding placed in the tin lid and light it. Hold carefully to prevent the flame from burning the paper sides and, when fully inflated, allow the balloon to rise slowly, holding on to the base for a few seconds before finally letting it go.

A SEASIDE SAND WAGON.

Those readers who want to make a useful toy for the younger ones of the family will like to make the sand wagon shown at Fig. 1. It will be seen that this toy is formed by fitting rollers to a shallow box. It is the only form of waggon of any real use on soft sand and will give pleasure to the little one who uses it.

Begin by making the shallow box first, a convenient size would be 10 in. by 6 in. by 2 in. The wood need not be more than $\frac{1}{4}$ in. thick, but for rough wear the sides could be made of $\frac{3}{8}$ in. material, the bottom only of $\frac{1}{4}$ in. wood. The ends need not be more than nailed, although dovetail joints would add to the appearance.

It will be seen at Fig. 2 that the rollers are about the same distance from the bottom as the height of the sides, it is not an important matter and anything from 2 in. to 4 in. will do. The rollers should be at least 1 in. diameter and can be cut from a broomstick.

The supporting brackets should be of strip iron $\frac{1}{4}$ in. by $\frac{1}{8}$ in. If the rollers are home made, the method to be followed in working out the round is shown at Fig. 4, the wood is first planed square, next it is marked on the ends to form an octagon as at B. The length is now planed down to the shape at C and finally to the round at D. Sufficient

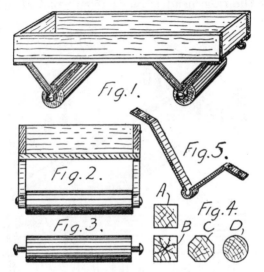

Fig. 1.

Fig. 2.

Fig. 3.

Fig. 4.

Fig. 5.

A.

B. C. D.

material should be prepared to cut the two lengths. The lengths of iron should be first bent over in the centre to allow of a large round headed screw being placed through; the sides are bent outwards, flattened at the top to the required slope and drilled to take screws. Finish with paint or varnish and drive a stout screw eye at one end.

A SAND RAKE.

The sand rake shown at Fig. 1 will be welcomed by the little ones and many readers will like to

make one or two for the tiny-tots to use when
playing on the beach. A useful size would be a
length of 7 in. with a handle about 15 in. long, but
the actual dimensions are a matter of choice.

The method of construction is quite simple,
first the rake head is made from wood about $\frac{3}{4}$ in.

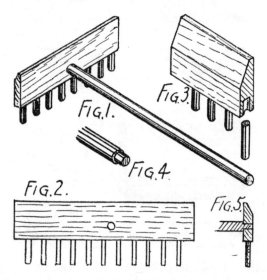

FIG. 1.

FIG. 3.

FIG. 4.

FIG. 2.

FIG. 5.

thick, planed to $\frac{5}{8}$ in. and then the prongs, cut from
birch dowelling, are fitted in holes drilled in the
head. A section of the head with the pegs or
prongs in position is shown at Fig. 3. The lengths
of dowelling, about $\frac{1}{4}$ in. or $\frac{5}{16}$ in. diameter need not
project more than $1\frac{1}{2}$ in. or let into the head deeper
than 1 in. The bit used for boring the holes
should be carefully chosen so that it bores a hole
slightly smaller than the dowelling. The lengths
of the latter material can be glued in position, but

if they are carefully fitted it is not likely that they
will fall out, as the wood is sure to get sufficiently
damp enough to prevent them falling out.   A better
plan than gluing is to drive a fine brass pin through
each prong.

The handle can be of $\frac{3}{4}$ in. dowelling, and the end
should be cut smaller as at Fig. 4, and fitted tightly
in a suitable hole bored in the head.   To keep the
head in position a nail should be driven in from
the underneath.   A coat of size and varnish will
improve the appearance, but the wood should be
made thoroughly smooth with glasspaper.

HOW TO MAKE A PAIR OF STILTS.

Although not so commonly seen as they used to
be, stilts are quite amusing to use and with a little
practise it is possible to obtain a considerable
degree of facility in their use.   The wood used can
be round, but it is simpler to use $1\frac{1}{4}$ in. or so
square section wood.   The wood should be
straight and free from large knots at least,
although it is better to have the wood with a
straight even grain.

It will be seen at Fig. 1, that the top of the stilt
is rounded to form a handle, the height of the
stilts is not important so long as the distance between the top and the footrest is the same as the
distance from the elbow and foot of the user.
Generally it will be found convenient to make the
length equal to the distance between the shoulder
and the foot.

The height of the footrest from the ground should

be from 1 ft. to 2 ft. ; it is not advisable to have a greater distance than this. The best method of securing the foot rest to the upright is shown at Fig. 2 and consists of cutting the footrest to a slope and cutting a corresponding notch into the upright.

The footrest should be the same thickness as

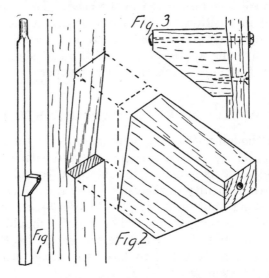

the upright, about 3½ in. or so in length and 2½ in. to 3 in. deep. Two long screws can be used to secure the footrest to the upright, but if a bolt can be fitted as shown at Fig. 3, the stilts will be very much stronger.

The rounded portion on the top of the upright can be done with a spokeshave, but the wood should be finished smooth with glasspaper to prevent the formation of splinters.

CUTTING LETTER STAMPS IN LINO.

Initial letters and monograms are easily made for printing purposes in fairly thick cork linoleum. In making a block of the letter A as shown at Fig. 1,

first draw out the letter full size and transfer it to the cleaned surface of a piece of lino of suitable size.   All the ground is cut away leaving the border and letter standing out as at Fig. 2.   The next step is to cut along the edges of the letter, as at

Fig. 3, with a cut which slopes towards the letter, the knife must not on any account undercut the lines. When the outlining has been done, and the knife must be kept sharp to do it, the background may be peeled off in thin lino and cut away with a gouge in thick material, the former method

is shown at Fig. 4. Although the work is not difficult, considerable care is needed to avoid cutting into the letter or border.

Monograms and all kinds of simple ornaments may be done in this way and it will be possible with a little practice to make some nice pictorial illustrations.

To make a print, obtain some good printer's ink, a roller and absorbent paper as used in cyclos-style work. The ink can be spread with a brush, the paper should be slightly damp and is best placed between some damp bloting paper. Press the paper on the block, rub it over with the roller, or if not, place a second dry sheet on top and rub over it with a hard pad ; one may be made with a circle of wood covered with stiff paper.

MAKING CHRISTMAS CARDS.

There are several ways of making Christmas cards ; one is to paint some sprays of holly and mistletoe on a piece of stout drawing paper and then to print the greeting in good lettering. Another way is to design and cut a stencil and make a number of cards all alike.

Any stiff paper can be used for the stencil, note-paper coated with linseed oil and allowed to dry answers very well. A third method is to use rubber type which can be bought in small boxes, glue them on a piece of plywood and print the cards. A simple way of making printed cards is to choose a suitable greeting, arrange it with your name and address and use an ordinary inking pad. Added interest can be given by an illustration of a spray of leaves or a simple pattern cut out of linoleum. In this way a picture block can be made. The design should be drawn on a piece of linoleum which should be rubbed down quite smooth and flat with fine glasspaper, and the back built up to the same thickness as the rubber type with paper or cardboard glued on. The design is drawn on with pen or pencil and cut out with a sharp knife and glued on in position on the ply-wood base. In order to get type and decoration quite level, the block should be placed on a piece of fine glasspaper and gently rubbed on it. The best way to ink it is to use printer's ink which can be obtained from any printer for a trifle, and apply it with a roller made by fitting a length of inner tube from a cycle tyre on a short piece of round wood and arranging a wire handle; it is quite easy to make. Place some of the ink on a piece of glass or slate, spread it with the roller and then run the roller over the block just before it is pressed down on the paper; drawing paper is best. Several thicknesses of blotting paper should be placed under the paper and the block pressed down hard.

A BOOK TO HOLD HOLIDAY SNAPSHOTS.

A book similar to that shown at Fig. 1 can be easily and inexpensively made with stiff brown paper and cardboard. Glazed linen, bookbinder's cloth and vegetable parchment are useful for covering but they cost a little more.

First cut two pieces of cardboard 7 in. by 4¼ in. and cover one side with paper or cloth, allowing

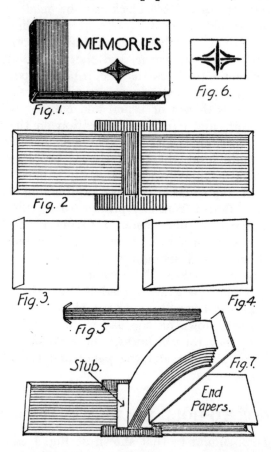

Fig. 1.

Fig. 6.

Fig. 2

Fig. 3.

Fig. 4.

Fig 5

Stub.

Fig. 7.

End Papers.

the material to overlap about ½ in. on the inside. Next cut a 4¼ in. by ¾ in. piece of cardboard and paste it, with the two covered pieces, on a piece of stout paper or cloth measuring 3½ in. by 6 in.

with $\frac{1}{8}$ in. between as at Fig. 2. Fold over the margin and place under pressure.

For the pages cut 24 pieces of brown paper each $7\frac{3}{4}$ in. by 4 in. and fold over one short edge, 1 in. wide, to serve as a stub, as at Fig. 3. Cover the stubs with paste in turn and lay the sheets, one on top of the other as at Fig. 4 and continue until the thickness at the back equals $\frac{3}{4}$ in., the width of the cardboard in the centre between the boards. Place under pressure and then place a stub in the underside as at Fig. 7. The lettering and decoration of the cover can now be done, if several books are made, a stencil can be cut as in Fig. 8.

The two outside stubs are now coated with paste, the covers placed in position and under pressure. To complete, fold two $13\frac{1}{2}$ in. by 4 in. sheets in half, to form end papers as at Fig. 7 and then paste one to the inside of each cover.

The bound book should now be placed under pressure and left until the paste has had sufficient time to dry. A book to hold picture post-cards or cigarette cards can be made in the same way.

SIMPLE BOOKBINDING.

Magazine numbers soon get lost if they are not kept in a special folder or case and even then are liable to disappear. The better plan is to sew the parts together on the completion of a volume and fit them with a cover. A simple method of doing this is illustrated at Fig. 1 and following drawings. In the first place covers are removed and wire staples, if any, carefully pulled out. Next they are placed in order with the earliest section on top, and then the sewing board prepared. This is a piece of wood larger than the size of the sheet with battens at each end. The next step is to provide some stiff braid or tape, wide linen tape will do if coated with glue and left to dry. The first section of the book is placed on the board

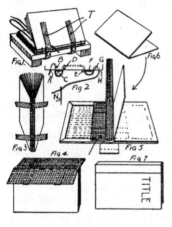

and about 8 in. of tape pinned to the front edge in such a position that about 1½ in. or so of the section is left outside, this is indicated at T, Fig. 1. Now provide a long needle, those used for crewel work are most suitable, and some linen thread, then commencing at the left hand end, push the needle through to the centre pages (these are opened out) as at A, Fig. 2. Pull the thread through to within 2 in. of the end and then bring the needle out again alongside the tape as at B, pass across the tape C and through the pages to D. The needle is now pushed through from inside to the front at E, alongside the second tape F, it is then carried back as at G, and is finally brought out at H. The next section is placed on top, opened out and the process reversed in order, and when the end is reached, the free end left at A is tied to the thread. A third section is now placed on top and the same procedure followed and this is repeated in each section until complete. The bound pages will appear as at Fig. 3, and at this stage the pages are placed under pressure, and if desired, the edges can be trimmed with a sharp knife. The next stage as at Fig. 4, consists in gluing on a strip of muslin or canvas to cover the back and also secure the tapes. The cover is made from two piece of cardboard slightly larger than the size of the pages and covered with some suitable material, bookbinder's cloth, casement cloth, vegetable parchment or paper, brown or coloured. The edge of the material is pasted on the inside of cover and sufficient space left to allow for the thickness of the back, the latter being covered with an extra strip if desired as at Fig. 5. The back is now placed in position and the two flaps glued or pasted down. The end papers, Fig. 6, are prepared to fit in between the covers and the pages, and then glued to the inside of the cover. The book is now placed under a weight to allow the paste to dry and then the volume is ready for the title as at Fig. 7.

FORMING A HOME MUSEUM.

There are very few homes where a number of curiosities of nature or of manufacture are not to be found and it is an interesting occupation to collect them together, label them, and add to the collection from time to time. It is interesting to keep mementos and records of holidays in this way, and readers who are keen of geology or nature study will like to keep the results of their labours in an accessible form.

The easiest method of arranging the museum specimens is to make a number of boxes with slip-in glass lids and arrange the boxes on shelves ; cardboard or thin wood partitions can be fitted in the boxes to suit the particular specimen. Scrap books can be adapted to hold dried leaves and flowers and shallow boxes with glass lids can be used to form collections illustrating the bark, leaves, flowers and the fruit of various trees.

Leaves and flowers pressed between sheets of blotting paper soaked in oxalic acid and dried, will retain their original colouring for a considerable time. Fruits can be varnished or preserved in alcohol. Ancient flints, Roman pottery and old coins are still obtainable and form the basis of interesting collections and the seashore will provide material for collections of all kinds of shells, pebbles, sea weed, flowers and plants.

The countryside provides opportunities for the geologist and botanist and the naturalist will find it a happy hunting ground for butterflies and moths.

Readers who are fond of drawing and photography can deepen their interest in their subject by making studies of antiquarian and architectural subjects and the neighbourhood of cathedral cities will provide plenty of material.

Drawings and photographs can be mounted in albums and placed on the museum shelves or they can be mounted by the passe partout method and hung on the walls close to the other exhibits.

Another method of collecting information of

interest is to cut out of the papers any item of interest relating to exhibits. These news cuttings can be pasted on cards and arranged in a file, or pasted in a special book.

The amateur photographer can add highly interesting exhibits to the home museum by series of photographs illustrating the growth of various plants at regular intervals. Pot plants are more suitable for this purpose than those growing in the garden as they can be taken against a plain background. Trees photographed at monthly intervals during a year will also form an interesting exhibit.

A CHEMICAL WEATHER GLASS.

Although not as reliable as a barometer, the weather glass shown at Figs. 1 and 2 is indicative of weather changes. When the liquid is clear, it will be fine and dry, when crystals form and gradually rise, stormy weather is indicated, when fern like formations are seen at the top, it is likely to be cold and stormy. The apparatus is composed of a 5 in. or 6 in. by $\frac{5}{8}$ in. test tube, two strips of thin metal and flannel, screws and a wood back. The back, A

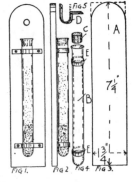

as at Fig. 3, should be of $\frac{1}{4}$ in. wood, $7\frac{1}{4}$ in. by $1\frac{3}{4}$ in., shaped at the top, bored with a hole for hanging and polished. The test tube, B, Fig. 4, should be fitted with a cork C, and two bands D, bent as at Fig. 5, so as to clip the tube to the back and drilled and lacquered. Strips of flannel as at E are wrapped round the tube under the clips. Make up the following solution : Camphor 1 dr., Potassium Nitrate $\frac{1}{4}$ dr., Ammonium Chloride $\frac{1}{4}$ dr., Absolute Alcohol 1 oz., Distilled Water 1 oz. The solution should be mixed or poured in a beaker or cup, placed in a bowl of hot water, thoroughly dissolve and mix the ingredients ; it is poured into the tube while warm, the tube is then corked and sealed with sealing wax.

A PENCIL AND KNIFE SHARPENER.

The little appliance illustrated below will be welcomed as an addition to the equipment of the writing desk. It is made from a 7 in. by 1 in. by

$\frac{1}{4}$ in. piece of wood with a strip of coarse emery cloth at one end and a strip of fine at the other. The narrow portion in the centre can be formed with a scribing gouge or with a half-round file. The other half should be covered with coarse and fine glasspaper. Both paper and cloth should be attached with glue and the work placed under pressure until dry.

A CLOTHES BRUSH RACK.

The rack shown at Fig. 1, although very simple in construction, makes an effective piece of furniture. The wood should be planed to 1 in. by $\frac{3}{4}$ in., and the dimensions made to suit the size of the brushes. A convenient size is to allow openings of 9 in. by 3 in. for the brushes and about 4 in. for the centre mirror. Mark out all the parts and cut the halving joints as at Fig. 2, and then form a rebate from the back as shown at Fig. 3, to take a bevelled edge mirror and a plywood back. The finished work should be oiled or polished before the hooks for the brushes are attached. Brass mirror plate or screw eyes can be used for hanging the rack against the wall.

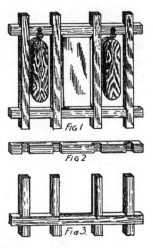

Fig I

Fig 2

Fig 3.

PIERCED METALWORK.

A Blotting Pad.

The blotting pad illustrated at Fig. 1 consists of a thick cardboard, millboard or ply wood base with corner pieces of metal, copper or brass of 18 gauge or pewter of 14 gauge can be used, but if it can be afforded, silver of 22 gauge is very suitable; the thickness is measured by S.W.G. (Imperial Standard Wire Gauge). The four metal plates are $3\frac{3}{8}$ in. square, but they can be set out on a piece measuring $6\frac{7}{8}$ in. square. The method of marking one of the plates is shown at Fig. 2, lines $2\frac{1}{2}$ in. and $2\frac{7}{8}$ in. being marked off from adjacent sides with the diagonal lines as shown. The pierced openings shown at Fig. 3 are set out from circles and then draw by hand; but to ensure accuracy a template of the required shape can be made and placed on the diagonal at each corner so that the marking point can be run around it. The openings can be sawn out with a fretsaw or a series of small

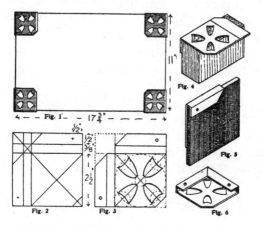

holes drilled close to the edge and then the metal can be filed to shape.

The outer corners should be cut to shape and holes to take small paper fasteners drilled as shown and the plate carefully cleaned and polished. The finest emery should be used for copper and then the finished surface worked by rubbing on pumice powder with a hard nail brush. A finer powder should be used for pewter, ordinary knife polish is suitable. Water of Ayr stone is used for silver and the final polish effected with rouge, applied with a wool mop or a soft rag. The method of bending the edges of the plates is shown at Fig. 4, the first stage being done on a hardwood block with a mallet. For the second stage as at Fig. 5, a metal plate equalling in thickness the base, plus sufficient for the blotting paper, should be provided, but a piece of hardwood can be used instead, although it will be rather difficult to obtain sharp edges. The joint can be soldered if desired, but is it not really necessary. The plates should be given another polish and if copper or brass are used they should be warmed and then coated with colourless lacquer which can be bought ready for use at most oil and colour shops ; it is applied with a camel hair brush. Keep the metal free from finger marks and not too hot to hold on the hand. The plates shown finished at Fig. 6 should be placed in position on the prepared base, the size shown at Fig. 1 is for a full size piece of blotting paper, and holes should be bored so that paper fasteners can be pushed through and turned over on the top of the base.

A SIMPLE METHOD OF FRAMING PICTURES.

One of the simplest and most effective ways of framing pictures is that known as the " Passe-Partout " and consists of pasting the picture on a piece of cardboard, placing a piece of glass over it and binding the two together by means of gummed strips of paper. Suitable binding strips can be obtained in black and some colours in rolls from a stationer, but generally it will be found that ordinary brown paper and tube glue will be suitable. The front of the picture is shown at Fig. 1, and the back at Fig. 2. First of all paste the picture on a suitable piece of cardboard with sufficient margin if it is to show a white mount, or within $\frac{1}{8}$ in. if framed up close. The mount if

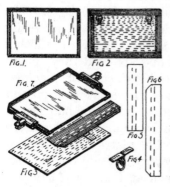

Fig. 1.   Fig 2.   Fig 6

Fig. 7.

Fig 5

Fig 4

Fig 3.

used should be of ordinary cartridge drawing paper with the picture opening neatly cut out. The glass should be exactly the same size as the cardboard and then the two main parts will be flush on the edges. The back, Fig. 3, is provided with holes for tapes, these hold small brass rings as at Fig. 4 ; the tape is allowed to project $\frac{1}{2}$ in. or so at the back, and is pasted down inside. The ends are now covered over with pieces, as at Fig. 5, overlapping the glass from $\frac{1}{4}$ in. to $\frac{1}{2}$ in. ; the amount of overlap at the back does not matter. The long edges are mitred at the front corners as at Fig. 6. Ordinary paper clips are useful in keeping the parts together while the strips are being secured.

A FOLDING HAT AND COAT RACK.

This is a simple piece of work, the only difficult part being the shaping of the pegs. Two strips are planed up to 1 ft. 10 in. by 1 in. by $\frac{1}{2}$ in. as at A and four lengths of the same width and thickness to 1 ft. The ends are rounded and holes are bored 10 in. apart as shown. A piece of wood measuring 2 ft. by 7 in. by ½ in. finished thickness

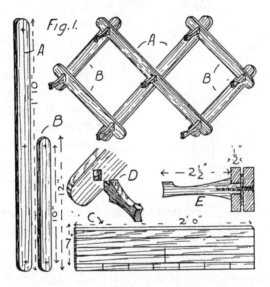

will be sufficient to make all the pieces as at C. The pegs can be of any suitable shape, they are tenoned into the strips as shown at D. The strips are fitted together with screws, but thin washers should be placed between the pieces as indicated in the section at E.

A BOOK TROUGH.

The Book Rest shown at Fig. 1 is a useful article for the table and offers opportunity for skill in the design and decoration of the ends. For those

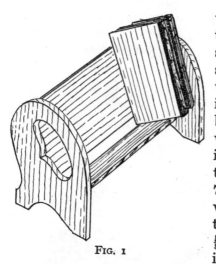

FIG. I

who can use the bow-saw and spoke-shave, the suggestion given will prove interesting work. It will be seen at Fig. 2, which is ruled out in 1 in. squares, that the height is 7 in. and the total width $6\frac{3}{8}$ in., the thickness should be $\frac{5}{8}$ in. or $\frac{1}{2}$ in., there is no need to make it thicker. The grooves should be very carefully marked out and it is here that the difficulty of the work lies. Unless both ends are exactly alike, it will be impossible to get the work to stand true on the table. The grooves should be taken down $\frac{1}{4}$ in. and the two pieces fitting in them about 10 in. or 12 in. long.

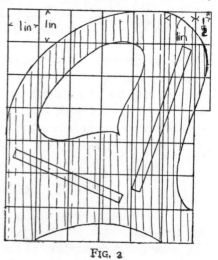

FIG. 2

EASILY MADE BOOKSHELVES.

The design at Fig. 1 can be made from any wood prepared to 6 in. wide and $\frac{3}{4}$ in. thick and if pur-

Fig. 1

chased machine planed, it is a piece of work that is suitable to make up at home with a few tools.

The various parts with sizes are shown at Fig. 2. The grooves for the shelves are shown carried right across the width of the wood, but a neater job can be done by stopping them $\frac{1}{4}$ in. from the front edge and making corresponding notches in the shelves.

The small locker at the bottom will be found useful for keeping odds and ends, as a lock can be fitted as shown.

Apart from the housing joint, there is nothing difficult in the construction and the work should appeal to beginners.

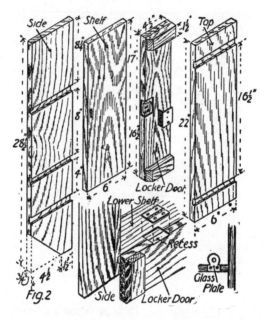

Fig.2

A CORNER BRACKET.

The bracket shown at Fig. 1 can be made from $\frac{1}{2}$ in. or $\frac{5}{8}$ in. wood to any reasonable size. A convenient set of dimensions would be 18 in. long by 7 in. wide for a bracket of medium size, but these sizes can easily be altered so long as the main proportions are not departed from.

The side view of the bracket without shelves is shown at Fig. 2, this illustration also shows the method of cutting out the brackets, which as will be seen, are let into grooves cut to a depth of about $\frac{1}{4}$ in. The method of shaping one of the sides is also indicated, due allowance must be made for the amount of the rebate so that both sides are alike. Shaping can be done with bow-saw, spokeshave and chisel, care being taken to clean up the edges quite smooth.

FIG. 1

The side shape shown at Fig. 2 is suggested as an alternative to that at Fig. 1, which may be found somewhat difficult by beginners.

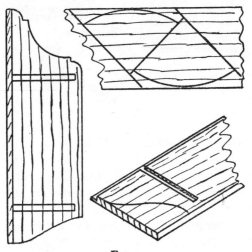

FIG. 2

HOW TO MAKE A FOLDING CHAIR.

In the chair shown at Fig. 1, known as a folding or deck chair, there are three frames made of hardwood planed to $1\frac{1}{4}$ in. by $\frac{7}{8}$ in. and slightly rounded on the corners. These frames are shown in Fig; 2 and numbered 1, 2 and 3. The rails joining them are shown in section A, B C and D. Frame 1 is

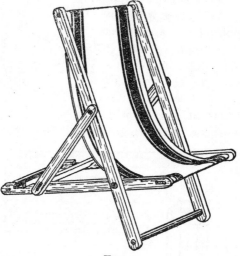

FIG. I

composed of two 48 in. lengths with a round rail A at one end of 1 in. diameter and a rail B, with rounded edges, $1\frac{1}{2}$ in. by $\frac{7}{8}$ in. The method of tenoning these rails in is shown to an enlarged scale at A and B. Wedges are used as shown to keep the tenons tight. Frame 2 is made with two lengths 40 in. long with a rail A at one end and another of the section at C at the other, this is

2 in. by $\frac{7}{8}$ in. with the corners planed off, they are both tenoned in as before and the completed frame should fit inside frame 1 leaving a space of $\frac{1}{8}$ in. each side. The lower end of the frame should be notched as at N, Fig. 3, either three or four notches being usual. No. 3 frame has two sides 22 in. long

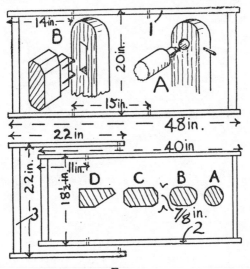

Fig. 2

with a rail of the section shown at D, it is 22 in. wide and allows of a space of $\frac{1}{8}$ in. each side of frame 1. The next step is to bore the holes as shown by the dotted lines at Fig. 2 and then rivet the lengths together as at E, Fig. 3. The rivets should be of iron $\frac{3}{8}$ in. diameter with washers $\frac{1}{8}$ in. thick. The method of hammering over the straight end of the rivet is shown at G, the round end of the rivet should be supported on a piece of lead or very hard wood. The canvas covering is tacked to the rails B and C, with the ends of the material doubled under as at H. Chair coverings can now be pur-

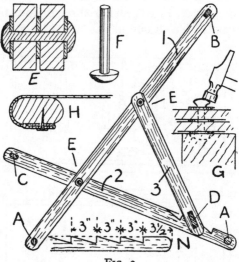

FIG. 3

chased which do not require nailing on, the cost is very little more and they are very satisfactory in use.

The wood can be rubbed down with glasspaper, sized and varnished to complete.

HOW TO MAKE A FOLDING TABLE.

The folding table at Fig. 1 is quite simple in construction and is strong enough for all ordinary purposes. The top can be of any wood planed to $\frac{1}{2}$ in. thick, but ply wood will be stronger and not liable to warp.   The various parts are shown at Fig. 2, which shows the table folded up in front, and side views.   The two rails B are 21 in. by $1\frac{3}{4}$ in. by $\frac{3}{4}$ in. the ends are rounded and the strips are screwed to the top to give a distance of $20\frac{1}{4}$ in. between.   The legs C are 33 in. by $1\frac{1}{4}$ in. by $\frac{7}{8}$ in.

FIG. I

and made in pairs, one pair is 20 in. wide and the other 18 in. wide.   The lower ends are joined with a cross rail D, planed to $1\frac{1}{2}$ in. by $\frac{1}{2}$ in. and dovetailed and screwed at the ends as shown in the detail at Fig. 3.   The width apart of the inner leg at the stop is kept to the required size with a strip of 1 in. square wood E, the method of forming the joint is shown in Fig. 3 to an enlarged scale. The widest pair of legs is screwed or rivetted to the rails B at F, and to strengthen both pairs

of legs, they are provided with strips G, planed to
$1\frac{1}{2}$ in. by $\frac{1}{4}$ in. The two pairs of legs are hinged
together with iron rivets half way up as shown
in the section at H. The method of fixing the
free pair of legs has now to be arranged, this is
effected by means of a stop J, into which the square

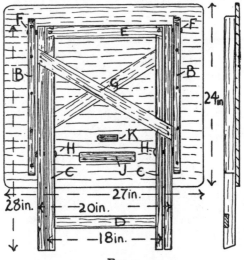

FIG. 2

top fits and it is retained in position by button K
which is screwed to the underside of the top. An
enlarged detail of this fitting is shown at Fig. 3.
The stop is composed of two pieces $\frac{1}{2}$ in. thick,
one piece is a trifle over 1 in. wide and the other,
fitting on it at right angles and parallel to the table
top is $1\frac{1}{2}$ in., both being 9 in. long. The bottom
should be 3 in. by 1 in. by $\frac{3}{4}$ in. The wood should
be cleaned up with glasspaper, sized and varnished.

Although a light table of this description should not be left out of doors, and exposed to the elements for any length of time, it will not come to much harm if it has been thoroughly well varnished.

A table designed to remain in the garden in all

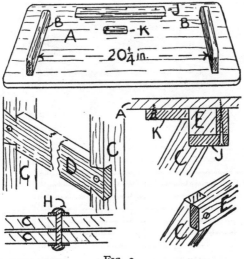

FIG. 3

weathers should be constructed differently with strong fixed legs, and a top made of strips of wood, with spaces between them, secured to strong battens or rails. For camping purposes, a folding table made to the above dimensions with a top, formed by $1\frac{1}{2}$ in. by $\frac{1}{2}$ in. strips with $\frac{1}{2}$ in. space between, will be found light enough, particularly if made of yellow pine. This timber is rather expensive, but is worth while when lightness is a consideration.

A SCRAPER MAT.

The mat shown at Fig. 1 is easily made from yellow deal batten and some lengths of old bedstead laths or similar material. The wood should

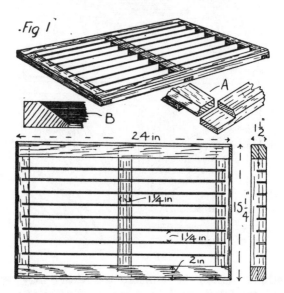

be planed to 2 in. by $1\frac{1}{2}$ in. and the corners joined by the lapped halving joint as at A. The lath is let into saw cuts, these are straight across the centre piece and at a slope on the two ends as shown in the section at B. The finished work should be painted at least three coats to preserve it from wet.

A PLATE RACK.

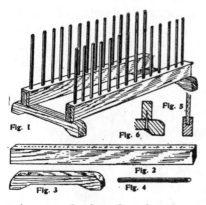

Fig. 1
Fig. 5
Fig. 6
Fig. 2
Fig. 3
Fig. 4

This is a simple piece of work as shown at Fig. 1, made with four pieces of deal and some lengths of $\frac{3}{8}$ in. dowelling. The two long lengths, Fig. 2, are 24 in. by $1\frac{3}{8}$ in. by 1 in., the feet are $8\frac{3}{4}$ in. by $1\frac{3}{8}$ in. by 1 in., and the dowels are cut to a length of $7\frac{1}{4}$ in. Mark a centre line along the long pieces, commence $1\frac{1}{4}$ in. from the end and set out lines $1\frac{3}{4}$ in. apart ; these give the centre of the holes which are bored with a bit providing a hole that is a tight fit for the dowels. The holes should be carried to a depth of $\frac{3}{4}$ in. The feet are shaped as at Fig. 3, the dowels cut off as at Fig. 4 and then glued in as at Fig. 5. The screws attaching the feet to the long lengths as at Fig. 5 should fit loosely in the feet but firmly in the long lengths.

A WINDER FOR WOOL.

Wool winders are made in several forms, one of the most useful being illustrated at Fig. 1. This piece of apparatus is screwed to the table and can be opened out to take any size of skein. The materials required are a large cotton reel, another smaller, a length of dowel rod or a wooden meat skewer of the same diameter as the hole in the reels and from 7 in. to 8 in. long, 24 lengths of 6 in. by ½ in. by ⅛ in. wood, a small bent galvanised iron G cramp and some wire nails. A large wooden crochet needle with a round knob on the end can be

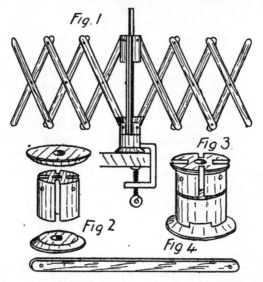

Fig. 1

Fig 2

Fig 3

Fig 4

used in place of the rod. The smaller reel should be fitted on the rod so that it is an easy fit, it is then sawn top and bottom to remove the flanges as at Fig. 2. The sides are divided into four equal parts, the line forming the centre of ⅛ in. grooves which are carried down as deep as possible without reaching the middle hole. Two methods can be followed in sawing out the grooves, one is to drill holes from end to end as close to the middle hole as possible and then saw to the line, the other is to make the saw cuts first and then cut out the waste with an $\frac{1}{8}$ in. chisel, the reel should be held in the vice while the sawing and chiselling is done. The method of treating the larger reel is shown at Fig. 3. First of all the bottom slot should be carried right through the wood as shown. This is easily done with a drill and cleaned out with an $\frac{1}{8}$ in. chisel. First of all measure the end of the cramp, and then provide a twist drill of the same diameter as the thickness of the cramp. The width of the end of the cramp is marked on the reel and holes are drilled at these points right through the wood. One or more holes should be drilled between in order to remove as much of the waste as possible, and then clean out the slot with a chisel. The upper portion of the reel is now slotted as indicated, holes can be drilled from the top and the waste removed with a chisel after suitable saw cuts have been made, the inside edges being cut square. The strips of thin wood should be made thoroughly smooth with glasspaper and the ends slightly rounded and then the holes as indicated at Fig. 4 should be drilled with a fine twist drill, a bradawl could be used, but the use of the drill prevents splitting. The pieces fitting in the middle should have holes at both ends. Four sets of trellis formation are now made, small wire nails being used as rivets and cut to the length with pliers. The ends of the strips which are to fit in the centre should be trimmed off and then each fitted in turn in the slots. Considerable care should be taken in fitting the trellis, suitable holes being made with a fine drill, and fine wire nails driven in. The rod is now secured to the bottom reel with glue, taking care that it does not go beyond the slot intended for the cramp. The best finish for the winder is a shellac varnish. The work could be French polished, but it would be necessary to do the work before the trellis work is rivetted up.

A RAFFIA AND CANE TABLE MAT.

The illustration shows a table mat which is most effective when worked with two colours in

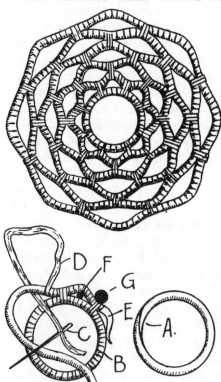

raffia. The commencement is in the form of a ring about 1 in. in diameter, spliced as at A and bound with raffia. A row of different coloured raffia covered cane is bound to this ring, the raffia is threaded through a needle C wrapped round the cane as at D, the latter being sliced off at the end as at E. A round peg is placed between the two rows of cane to act as a guide and carried round as the work proceeds. When the end of the round is complete, the cane is cut off at a slope to fit on the commencing piece E and finished off with raffia. The next round is done with a larger guide peg and continued in the same way, the same method being followed to complete the mat.

AN ICE-CREAM FREEZER.

There are few boys or girls who do not like ice-cream and therefore the ice-cream freezer illustrated at Fig. 1 will appeal to many readers. The particular advantage of the apparatus is that it can be made for a few pence by anyone who can do a little soldering. It will be seen by the section at Fig. 2 that two lever lid tins are required, one is of a large size and the other a few inches shorter and less in diameter. These tins are easily obtainable as they are the kind used more generally than those with a slip on lid. Those used by the writer were 10 in. deep and 6 in. diameter for the outer case and $8\frac{1}{2}$ in. by $3\frac{1}{4}$ in. for the inner case.

The first thing to do is to thoroughly clean them, but be careful not to use emery cloth or any abrasive that would remove the coating of tin. Next mark off the diameter of the smaller tin on the bottom of the larger one and proceed to cut a hole right through the bottom. This will probably be found the most difficult portion of the work as it must be neatly done. The inner tin is now soldered in position and to ensure that the inner case is parallel to the sides of the outer case, small blocks of wood should be placed inside to keep it in position during soldering. The handle and pin are made of galvanised wire soldered to a boss as at D, E, F and G. The base should be

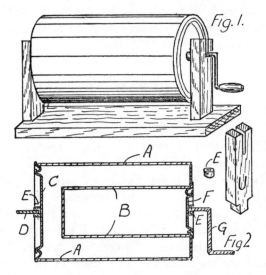

Fig. 1.

Fig 2

of ¾ in. wood with two slotted uprights, U, tenoned in as shown. The cream should be placed in the inner compartment and the freezing mixture in the outer and the latter revolved. Always wash out and thoroughly dry the tins immediately after use.

THE USE OF PLYWOOD.

There are many ways of using plywood and one method is to combine it with quarter section ball beading as shown at Fig. 1. A rebate is formed on the edge of the article, this rebate can be cut out of $\frac{3}{8}$ in. plywood as at Fig. 1, or thin plywood can be mounted on a base as at Fig. 2. The ball beading can be obtained already prepared from

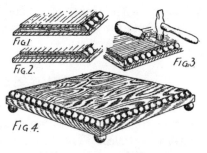

most cabinet-makers supply stores. The rebates should be worked as cleanly as possible and the beading carefully glued in. Small brads can be used to retain the beading as well, these will

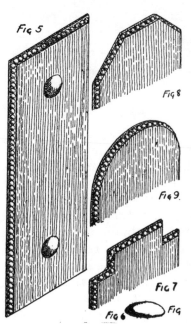

be necessary when doing circular work. The best method of driving the brads in is to use an old small triangular file mounted in a handle and hammer on the file as at Fig. 3, this is more suitable than a nail punch.

Tea-pot or flowerpot stands as at Fig. 4 are suitable for use with plywood. Similar material can be used for a finger-plate as at Fig. 5, the plain surface can be relieved with small flat bosses as at Fig. 6. Suggestions for different shapes are given at Figs. 7, 8 and 9.

A USEFUL STOOL.

The stool shown at Figs. 1 and 2 is useful as a seat in the house, as a footstool or as a stand for various articles. The only material required is a length of planed board, 9 in. by 1 in. The top at A, Fig. 2, measures 14 in. by 9 in., and is grooved in two places to take the legs as at B. These are

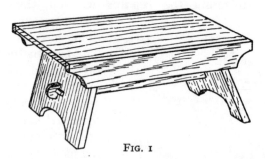

Fig. i

11 in. long and as they slope outwards, it will be necessary to make the grooves to suit. The distance from the end for the grooves should be about 3 in. and in order to obtain the correct slope of the sides of the groove, a bevel should be set to the correct angle ; this can be obtained from a large scale or full size drawing of the side elevation as shown at Fig. 2. The saw should be used at an angle to correspond with the slope, and care will be required when cutting out the waste, to avoid damaging the undercut side of the grooves.

The legs should be cut off top and bottom to the corresponding angle and the curved hollow at the bottom marked out, sawn with a bow saw and finished with a spokeshave. The slot for the stretcher must be left until the material has been

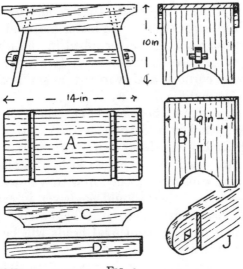

Fig. 2

prepared and it will be found that a 14 in. length of the wood will cut out two $3\frac{1}{4}$ in. wide pieces for the sides C, and leave a strip of about $2\frac{1}{4}$ in. for the stretcher D. If this is planed down to 2 in. wide, it will do for the stretcher. The tenon on the end should be full width and $\frac{3}{8}$ in. thick. The slot in each leg can now be marked out and cut to these dimensions.

The next stage is to make the two side pieces

which should be planed up to 3 in. wide and the ends shaped with a hollow curve as shown at C. The corners should be cut off with the saw and finished with chisel or plane, but the curved end looks much better and can be made with a spokeshave or large scribing gouge.

When all parts are made, they should be cleaned up with glasspaper, but the latter material should be used over a block and rubbed in the direction of the grain. Care must be taken to avoid rubbing down the corners and without a sand-papering block, this is difficult to avoid.

The legs should be placed into the groove, the stretcher fitted in and the side pieces attached to the top first with either screws or nails. If the former are used, bore holes with a bradawl or gimlet, and countersink the top with a suitable bit. If nails are used they should be driven in carefully and the heads driven in just below the surface with a nail punch; thin oval brads will be found most convenient.

The stretcher can now be wedged up tight, but care must be taken not to tighten it up too much or else the end of the tenon will split. Complete the nailing or screwing of the side pieces and then size and varnish the work. If it should be found that the stool does not rest firmly when placed on the level bench top or table, the best way is to pack it up with pieces of cardboard and to place a ruler on the table close up to the legs; by running a pencil round, a new line for either sawing or trimming with a chisel, can be formed.

A FIREPLACE SCREEN.

There is a difference between a fire-screen and a fire-place screen, although it is usual to call all fitments made for placing in front of the fireplace, fire screens. The fire-place screen is used in summer to form a decorative feature in front of

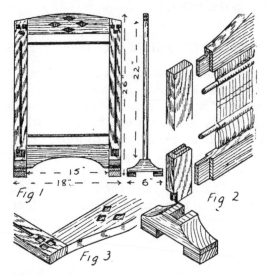

the grate, there are innumerable designs to be seen in furniture shops. The design shown at Fig. 1 is not difficult to make and consists of a framework decorated on the front, filled in with some suitable material and supported on two stout feet. The details of the joints are given at Fig. 2 and it will be seen that the top and bottom rails of the frame are tenoned into the uprights, the uprights are tenoned into the feet and the material is supported on two lengths of dowelling which fit in holes bored into the uprights. A suitable form of decoration is inlay as suggested at Fig. 3, but any suitable means of forming a simple decorative design will answer. As the work is more suitable for the more advanced of our readers, detailed description of the methods of setting out the work and cutting the joints is omitted.

A USEFUL STOOL FOR THE FIRESIDE.

The stool shown partly finished at Fig. 1 is not at all difficult to make and when finished will be welcomed at home. It is made from wood planed to $\frac{5}{8}$ in. thick, the best wood to use is oak, but as it may be a little too difficult to work, yellow deal can be used instead. The ends shown at Fig. 2 are finished to $10\frac{1}{4}$ in. by 10 in. and the top at Fig. 3 is 15 in. by 10 in. The best way to prepare these parts is to mark them off on a length of 11 in. by $\frac{3}{4}$ in. machine planed board, setting off one 15 in. and two $10\frac{1}{4}$ in. lengths with a little waste left at the ends and between each piece. The stopped groove on the end pieces is marked off 2 in. up, $\frac{5}{8}$ in. wide and $8\frac{1}{2}$ in. long. The top corners are notched out $\frac{1}{4}$ in. down and $\frac{3}{4}$ in. along. The curve is $1\frac{1}{2}$ in. high and drawn to within $1\frac{1}{2}$ in. of the sides. The stopped grooves on the top are 1 in. from the ends, $8\frac{1}{2}$ in. long and $\frac{5}{8}$ in. wide. The grooves should be cut to $\frac{1}{4}$ in. deep before the pieces are sawn apart, but great care should be taken that they are exactly the same width as the thickness of the wood, remembering that a little

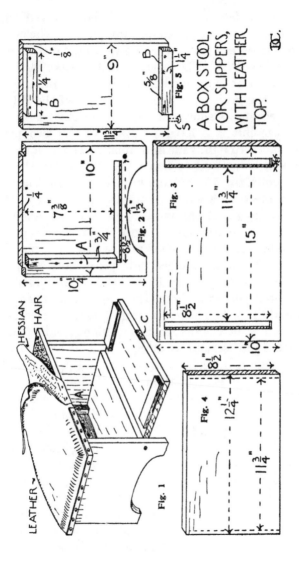

Fig. 5

B 7¼"

⅛"

6"

B ¼"

⅝"

11¾"

A BOX STOOL, FOR SLIPPERS, WITH LEATHER TOP.

Fig. 2

10"

¼"

7⅞"

A 3¾"

8½"

1½"

10¼"

Fig. 3

11¾"

15"

8½"

10"

Fig. 4

8½"

12¼"

11¾"

HESSIAN

HAIR

LEATHER

Fig. 1

C

of the surface of the wood will be removed when
cleaning up with the smoothing plane. The curves
should be cut with a bow-saw and finished with
a spokeshave. The bottom of the stool is shown
at Fig. 4, it is finished at $12\frac{1}{4}$ in. by $8\frac{1}{2}$ in. and will
fit in the grooves in the ends. One of the sides is
hinged and is shown at Fig. 5, the other is similar
in size but is a fixture. Each of the two pieces
is planed to 9 in. wide and finished $11\frac{3}{4}$ in. long, but
it will be as well to leave the actual length until
the ends, top and bottom have been glued together.
The piece of wood $\frac{3}{4}$ in. square in section at A is
$7\frac{1}{8}$ in. long and one piece is glued and bradded to
each end to provide a support for the fixed side.
The two pieces at B need not be fitted on, but they
will prevent the hinged side piece from warping;
these pieces $7\frac{1}{4}$ in. by $1\frac{1}{4}$ in. by $\frac{5}{8}$ in. are glued and
screwed on $\frac{1}{8}$ in. from the top. The fixed side
should now be cleaned up and glued in after being
carefully fitted and then the hinged side secured
with $1\frac{1}{2}$ in. screws as at S, the holes are bored in
the ends $\frac{5}{16}$ in. below the bottom and $\frac{7}{16}$ in. from the
edge. The best method of fastening the hinged
side is to use a ball catch, these can be bought very
cheaply in small sizes. The ball plate should be
let in the top and the striking plate on the door as
at C. If the wood is oak, it should be polished
with beeswax and turpentine, if deal, it can be
stained and polished or painted. The top is now
padded with curled horse hair which can be bought
at any upholsterers, a layer of about 3 in. high will
be sufficient. The material should be covered
with hessian, a kind of canvas used by upholsterers,

and pulled tightly over the stuffing and tacked to the edges of the wood. A long knitting needle is useful in distributing the hair so as to form an even pad. The leather, which may be rexine or pegamoid can be obtained at the same shop as the stuffing, should not cost very much as scrap pieces left over from a chair will be obtainable. The edging is a kind of gimp, this also with suitable leather covered nails can be obtained from the upholsterer.

Care should be taken in fitting the leather top to avoid creases, the corners especially must be carefully done ; it is impossible to avoid a crease or two here, but if the material is pulled down tightly, the work can be left quite neat.

MAKING GARDEN EDGING WITH CONCRETE.

There is plenty of scope for the energies of the young craftsman in the use of cement, either combined with sand or with an aggregate of gravel or coke-breeze in the form of concrete. This material was used to a considerable extent by the Romans, but it is only in comparatively recent times that it has been largely used in building.

Concrete is not difficult to make and it may be put to a vast number of uses in the home and the garden. A particularly useful method of using concrete is in making garden edging in the form of thin slabs, as at Fig. 1, cast in a wooden mould as at Fig. 2. Suitable dimensions for the slab should be determined upon, say 18 in. by 6 in. by $1\frac{1}{4}$ in., and then the mould is made with fairly stout wood. As it will be necessary to lock the ends of the slabs, an angle joint should be formed on the ends as at Fig. 3 and due allowance for this must be made in making the mould. First prepare a base of 1 in. planed wood to $18\frac{1}{2}$ in. by 8 in. and nail on two side strips each $18\frac{1}{2}$ in. by $1\frac{1}{4}$ in. by 1 in. as at Fig. 4. The two end pieces are made as at Fig. 5, using wood similar to that used for the sides. The

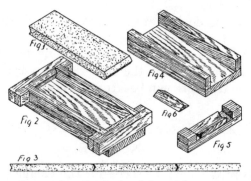

V-shaped opening is formed by $\frac{5}{8}$ in. square wood planed down to the diagonal. The length of the end pieces should be at least 12 in., with 2 in. blocks nailed on at the ends, and the V-shaped pieces cut to 6 in. long and securely nailed in position. The end with the hollow is formed by nailing on a 6 in. by $1\frac{1}{4}$ in. by $\frac{5}{8}$ in. triangular piece as at Fig. 6.

The concrete is made by mixing 1 part of cement with 2 parts of clean sand and 3 parts of stone, gravel or ballast. A cheaper form of concrete can be made with 5 parts of coke-breeze mixed with 1 part of cement. A wooden box measuring about

12 in. length, width and depth will form a good measure, guesswork should not be indulged in. The stone, gravel, ballast or breeze is termed the aggregate and it can be formed in addition to the materials mentioned, of granite, marble chips, or of broken flint.

The mixing should be done on a large board rather than on the ground and the cement should be thoroughly incorporated with the other material. Water is poured over the mixture with a watercan fitted with a rose, and then thoroughly mixed together with a spade. When the mixture is wet enough to hold together without excess of water, it should be poured into the moulds, several of them being convenient, and the top levelled off with a trowel. Just sufficient concrete should be made to fill the moulds.

Another method of forming the edging is to peg down two parallel boards about 1½ in. apart along the edge of the path and to pour the concrete in the space.

EASILY MADE CONCRETE FENCING.

The making of a garden fence, apart from the work of fitting up the necessary moulds, is no more difficult than that involved in making edging. A satisfactory fence can be made with slabs of concrete, made to any convenient size, cast in a flat shallow box and fitted between grooved posts made to the section shown at Fig. 7. The completed mould is shown at Fig. 8, and is arranged so that the casting takes the form shown in the section at A, and when removed is similar to the sketch at Fig. 9.

Begin by planing up two side pieces to 1 in. thick, the length should be at least 4 in. longer than the required post, but the width should be the same as the post. The two inside strips shown in

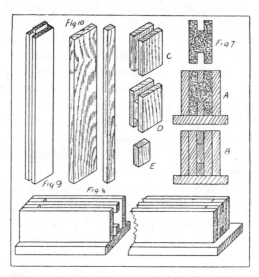

the section at B should be the same thickness as the slabs which are intended to fit inside the grooves and the width should be about ⅓ of the total width of the posts. The two end pieces should be made of three pieces as at C, D and E, the widths should be 2 in., the height of the side pieces the same as the long sides, the middle piece equal to the difference between the long strips and the side pieces; the thickness of the outer pieces as at C is made to at least the same as the inner strips, they can with advantage be made thicker. The long ones are kept together with a clamp as in Fig. 2 (see page 92). The slabs to fit between the upright posts can be from 2 ft. to 3 ft. long, but due allowance must be made for the depth to which the posts are placed in the ground in determining the width of the slabs. If more than one slab is required, the joining edges should be angle jointed as described in the first article mentioned above.

The material for the posts should be made of fine aggregate and an increased proportion of cement, but the slabs can be made of breeze as comparatively little strength is required. Greater strength can be obtained in the latter by using wire netting, stretched centrally in the mould. A good method of doing this is to have two end or side pieces with the netting in between: the concrete must cover the netting entirely.

A FLOWER POT IN CONCRETE.

The flower pot shown at Fig. 1 is made in a mould with a centre core, as shown at Fig. 2, but before it can be made it will be necessary to prepare a working drawing of the pot, as indicated at Fig. 3. It will be seen that there are certain recesses on each side—these are formed by tacking on strips of wood on the sides of the mould, as shown in the portion of the inside of the mould. First of all prepare two sides as shown at Fig. 2 ; these are 14 in. long, 11 in. wide, and $\frac{3}{4}$ in. thick. At each end nail or screw on stiffening strips of $1\frac{1}{4}$ in. by $\frac{3}{4}$ in. wood, 11 in. long, as indicated. The

remaining pair of sides are 11 in. in height in the
direction of the grain, 10 in. wide and $\frac{3}{4}$ in. thick,
and are strengthened at the back by means of
two strips of 2 in. by 1 in. wood $8\frac{1}{2}$ in. long.   The
next step is to prepare the four lengths of $\frac{1}{2}$ in.
square wood for the rim as indicated ; these are

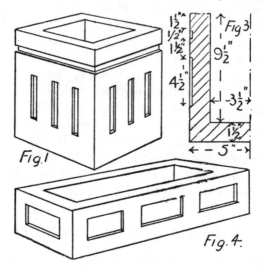

Fig.1

Fig. 4.

slightly bevelled towards the outside so as to come
away from the cement easily.   Each piece should
be 10 in. long and mitred to an angle of 45 degrees
at each end, and nailed to the sides exactly $1\frac{1}{2}$ in.
up from the base as shown.   Next prepare twelve
$4\frac{1}{2}$ in. by $\frac{1}{2}$ in. by $\frac{3}{8}$ in. strips slightly bevelled in
the same way, and tack them in their correct
position each side as shown.   The sides are now
ready, and we have next to prepare the base and
core, as shown at Fig. 2.   The base is 14 in. long,
$11\frac{1}{2}$ in. wide (11 in. will do), and $\frac{3}{4}$ in. thick, with

strips of $1\frac{1}{4}$ in. by $\frac{3}{4}$ in. stuff fastened on each end, as on the sides. The core is 7 in. square at the base, and $6\frac{7}{8}$ in. at the top, and $9\frac{1}{2}$ in. high. It is made of $\frac{3}{4}$ in. wood nailed together. It is an advantage, although not a necessity, to mitre the edges, and avoid the grain showing, as it is apt

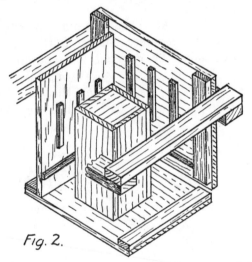

Fig. 2.

to become rough as the cement sets, with the continual moisture wood is bound to absorb. The sides are held together by means of the outside frame shown; this is made of 2 in. by 1 in. stuff, the inside measurements being 14 in. by $11\frac{1}{2}$ in. It is held in place by a couple of wedges placed underneath on the open sides.

An alternative design is shown at Fig. 4, the method of forming the mould is similar to that at Fig. 2, and will be found simple enough.

A good concrete mixture for flower pots of this

description is made by mixing together four parts of gravel or crushed stone, two parts of fine washed sand, and one part of cement made up on the mixing board, composed of lengths of floor board with a rim of 2 in. square wood nailed on. It should be fairly wet so that it will work well down into the mould.

Care should be taken that the mould is not taken apart until the concrete has set fairly hard, and the work should be covered with damp canvas or sacking until the cement has thoroughly hardened.

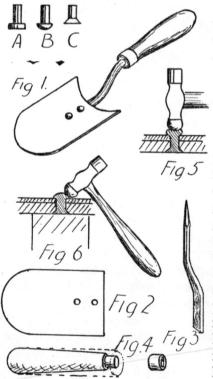

A B C

Fig 1.

Fig 5

Fig 6

Fig 2

Fig 4   Fig 3

A GARDEN TROWEL.

This is a simple piece of metalwork which can be put to good use in the garden. The finished piece of work is shown at Fig. 1 and consists of a shaped piece of sheet iron or steel, a length of $\frac{1}{4}$ in. iron rod and a length of broom

handle with a brass ferrule. Begin by cutting
the sheet of iron or steel to shape as at Fig. 2,
a useful size would be 6 in. by 5 in. with a
semi-circular end. The $\frac{1}{4}$ in. round rod should
be about 7 in. long with 3 in. flattened, bent
from the flat portion and the end pointed as at
Fig. 3. The handle, as at Fig. 4, can be shaped
from a piece of round wood $1\frac{1}{4}$ in. diameter, the
end shaped down and fitted with a $\frac{5}{8}$ in. length of
$\frac{5}{8}$ in. or $\frac{3}{4}$ in. brass tube. Of the three forms of
rivet in general use, as at A, B and C, the latter
is most suitable, two suitable holes are drilled,
countersunk on the flat rod and then hammered
down first as at Fig. 5 and finally as at Fig. 6.

A GARDEN SEED FRAME.

The seed frame shown at Fig. 1 is not difficult
to make and will be welcomed by the gardener who
wishes to raise seeds quickly without a hotbed.
Dimensions are not important, a useful size is a
length of 24 in., a width of 16 in., and a total
height of 9 in. with a slope of 3 in. to the sides.
The end pieces should be of fairly stout material,
1 in. would not be too thick, they should be planed
true to the shape. Join the ends with a $2\frac{3}{4}$ in.
by $1\frac{1}{4}$ in. length let in the top and screwed down,
but the sides should be planed to form the rebate
shown. Instead of planing the rebate which may
be found too difficult, the projecting pieces can be
nailed on a length, $1\frac{1}{2}$ in. by $1\frac{1}{4}$ in. in section.
The sides need not be more than $\frac{1}{2}$ in. thick and
nailed directly to the ends, as at Fig. 3, but the

top edges should be on a line with the fillets at A which are screwed on the inside of the ends to support the glass top, as at Fig. 4. The handle

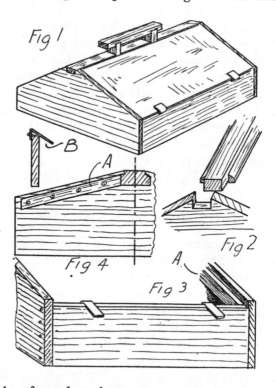

Fig 1

B

A

Fig 4

A.

Fig 2

Fig 3

can be of wood as shown, or an ordinary door pull can be screwed on. The glass should be cut to fit in the rebate formed by the fillets on the ends and the top piece and should rest on the sides, but to keep the pieces from slipping down, two pieces of thin sheet zinc about $\frac{3}{4}$ in. wide and 2 in. long should be fitted on as at B, and at Fig. 3.

These pieces of zinc are folded over on top of the glass as at Fig. 1. The sides and top can be kept in position with beading or brads. The wood should be painted at least three coats of good oil paint before the frame is used. If a frame of a larger size is required, it is better to divide the glass top in two parts with a length of sash-bar ; this material can be purchased prepared ready for use.

A GARDEN SWING.

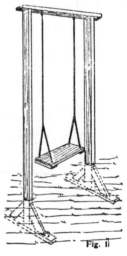

Fig. 1

A swing should be soundly constructed and made of well seasoned timber. The usual design is shown at Fig. 1 and comprises two uprights of 5 in. by 3 in. timber varying from 6 ft. to 8 ft. in height. The method of forming the base, which is below the surface as at Fig. 1, is illustrated to an enlarged scale at Fig. 2. The upright A is tenoned into a base B, which should be about 2 ft. 6 in. long at least and of the same material as the uprights. The struts C are tenoned to the base and the uprights, and should be about 18 in. long ; they can be nailed by cutting the ends to a mitre as at Fig. 3, but the better way is to form stub tenons on the ends as at Fig. 4. A section of the joints is shown at Fig. 5. The top piece should be about 3 ft. long and the same width and thickness as the uprights, the top of the uprights being tenoned in

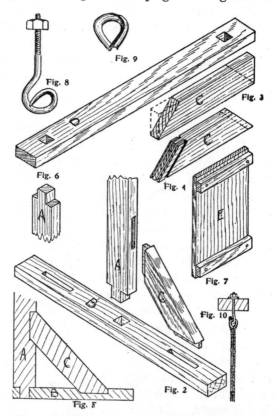

as at Fig. 6. The seat is formed with a board of suitable size with cross battens screwed underneath as at Fig. 7, holes being bored for the ropes. The best form of hook is illustrated at Fig. 8, this kind is much safer than the ordinary hook.

The thimble shown at Fig. 9 is used to prevent wear on the rope and is used as in the diagram at Fig. 10. The whole of the work should be thoroughly treated with wood preservative, particular care being taken with that portion of the wood which is placed below the surface.

Owing to the strain thrown on to the framework of a swing, it is essential that the constructional work should be done in an exceedingly workman-like manner, no part of it should be scamped.

In securing the frame in position, the two holes in the ground should be dug out to the required depth for the feet and then the bottom members carefully levelled, not by raising up the lowest, but by deepening the hole in which the highest side rests. The soil should be returned to the hole a little at a time and thoroughly rammed down, failure to do this part of the work properly may cause the struts to give way and weaken the frame.

HOW TO MAKE A LEVER TWIG CUTTER.

A handy little implement suitable for cutting all sorts of twigs which are beyond the reach of hand clippers is shown at A, it can be used for trimming trees and gathering fruit and will be found of great use. The long support should be of round wood about 1 in. diameter or stouter if over 6 ft. or 8 ft. in length, ash is most suitable, but the wood must be free from knots.

The flat shape of the curved cutter is shown at B and should be about 3 in. across the inside of the curve, the other portions being in proportion.

The lever cutter is made of a straight piece and ground on the opposite side to the ground inner edge of the curve. Thin sheet steel can be used for the portion at B, but the straight piece at C should be of stouter material. The two parts are rivetted together and act in the same way as

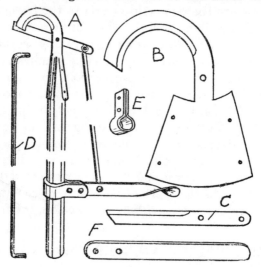

a pair of shears, except that one only of the cutting blades is moved. The operating lever is connected with the cutting lever with a length of iron rod as at D, this is bent at both ends and is fitted in holes and secured either by burring over the ends or by running a thread on them and fitting on an ordinary nut.

The clip to hold the operating lever is shown at E and fits securely to the pole, the lever at F is cut out straight at first and is then bent by heating and twisting.

Actual dimensions have been omitted as the work is sufficiently simple to provide an interesting problem for the metalworking craftsman. The curved cutter will probably be the only part requiring thought in working out, but with a suitable piece of steel, a punch and hacksaw, little real difficulty should be experienced. The cone shaped base which fits on the end of the pole will provide a nice piece of simple forge work, but it can be done with the aid of a fire, a length of gas barrel and a hammer. The cutting edges should be hardened and tempered.

GARDEN BASKETS.

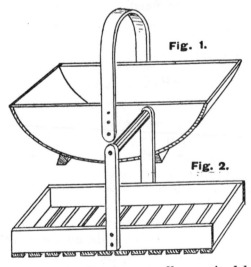

Fig. 1.

Fig. 2.

Some sort of basket is generally required by the gardener for the reception of weeds or the carrying of plants. One of the most effective baskets is the adaptation of the " Trug " as shown at Fig. 1. This handled box, as it really is, can be quite easily made from an old cheese box, or if not available, the material can be supplied by using ¾ in. wood for the sides and thin threeply wood for the curved base. The handle can be made of thin ash, steamed and bent to shape. The cross pieces at the bottom are required to keep the basket level. The curved wood should be nailed at frequent intervals.

The flat handled tray at Fig. 2 is quite a simple piece of construction, the sides should be from 2 in. to 3 in. wide and about ½ in. thick. They are nailed to end pieces of similar width and thickness. The bar across the bottom should be about 1 in. by ⅜ in. and the handle composed of two sides about 1¼ in. by ½ in. with a length of 1 in. round screwed to the top.

GARDEN ARCHES.

The ordinary form of trellis garden arch as shown at Fig. 1 is quite simple to make and can be formed with 1¼ in. square lengths joined with plasterer's laths, which are easily procurable. In order to nail on the strips quite parallel and the same distance apart, a strip of wood should be used, this can be from 2 in. to 4 in. wide, depending on the size of the arch. However well this kind of arch is made, it never looks quite neat and probably the design illustrated at Fig. 2 will appeal to the careful workman. The method of building the arch is shown at Fig. 3, the square wood should be about 1¼ in. side, and round wood about ⅝ in. or

Fig. 1

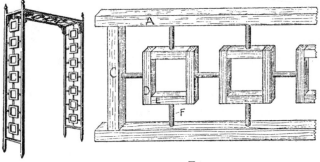

Fig. 2   Fig. 3

¾ in. diameter ; dowelling is useful for this purpose. Useful dimensions would be 7 ft. for the uprights A, 12 in. for the top and bottom pieces C, 8 in. for the pieces D, 5½ in. for those at E and 3 in. for the rounds at F. Several arches could be joined by uprights and tops made in a similar fashion to

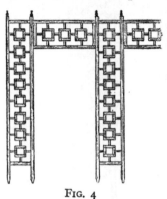

the arch as at Fig. 4, to form a pergola. Various adaptations of the above methods will s u g g e s t themselves to the en- thusiastic garden lover. The best finish for work of this kind is one of the wood preservatives such as solignum, but creosote will be found quite effec- tive and will give a

FIG. 4

pleasing colour to the wood after a little expos- ure to the weather.

It must be remembered that arches must be firmly fixed in the ground ; they offer considerable resistence to the wind, especially when covered with foliage. It is annoying to find that the wind has blown down a prettily covered arch and probably broken the branches. This can be pre- vented by placing the arch well into the ground and seeing that the wood which goes in the ground is thoroughly protected with creosote.

JOINTS FOR RUSTIC WORK.

So called rustic wood which is composed of round poles and branches, with or without the

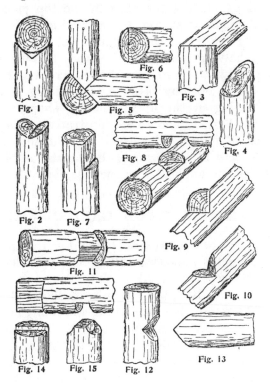

Fig. 1   Fig. 6   Fig. 3   Fig. 5   Fig. 4   Fig. 8   Fig. 2   Fig. 7   Fig. 9   Fig. 11   Fig. 10   Fig. 14   Fig. 15   Fig. 12   Fig. 13

bark, is a favourite material for making arches and fences in the garden. The method of jointing the round material is not so straightforward as in prepared wood, and the constructional work is of a rougher character. Fig. 1 shows the method followed when one piece is rested on the top of

another, a V-opening being cut as at Fig. 2. A
sloping piece can be fitted to an upright as at Fig. 3,
the sloping piece being cut as at Fig. 4. The joint
at Fig. 5 is a common one in rustic work and is
formed by cutting the ends of the top pieces to
a right angle as at Fig. 6 and resting them on a
notch on the top of the upright as at Fig. 7. The
lapped halving joint in rustic work is done as at
Fig. 8, or an alternative method is shown at Fig. 9,
a V-shaped opening being cut as at Fig. 10, the
piece fitting in the opening being shaped as at
Fig 11. Figs. 12 and 13 are illustrative of another
method of jointing the wood at right angles and
Figs. 14 and 15 are forms of the mortise and tenon
joint that are applicable to the material.

TWO EASILY MADE GARDEN SEATS.

The boy who stays at home for the greater
portion of his holidays, will probably be looking
for some constructional work that can be done
out-of-doors. Both the garden seats shown at Figs.
1 and 2 are intended for making and fixing in some
particular spot. Commencing with the plain seat
at Fig. 1, the first thing to do is to obtain suitable
material ; for the legs A and the cross rails B,
some 2 in. square deal can be used, but thicker
stuff, up to 3 in. is quite suitable.

The seat strips should be at least $1\frac{1}{4}$ in. thick for
a seat 6 ft. long, if longer the thickness of the wood
must be increased in proportion. The legs should
be 2 ft. 6 in. long and the rails about 14 in. or so,
this will allow of five 2 in. wide seat strips with 1 in.

between or five $2\frac{1}{2}$ in. wide strips equally spaced apart.

First form the mortise and tenon joints as at Fig. 3, and then let the legs into the ground, leaving about 3 in. overlap at each end. The top surface of the rails should be kept to the same level and this

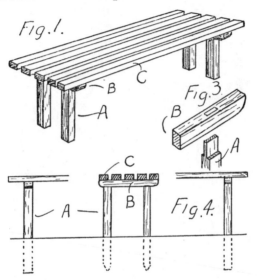

Fig. 1.

Fig. 3.

Fig. 4.

can be done if the holes in the ground are not quite so deep as the length of wood which goes in the ground, both pieces can then be driven in firmly to the correct height above ground. In order to fully protect the wood, the portion to enter the ground should be coated with creosote or tar.

The seat rails should be planed quite smooth, the wood can be obtained from a timber yard machine-planed ready for use, it will only require smoothing over with a plane, but the corners should be taken off to prevent the formation of splinters. When the strips have been nailed on, the heads of the nails should be carefully punched down well below the surface. To complete the work apply at least two coats of paint, but if the wood is kept quite clean during the construction a coat of size,

followed by varnish, will be effective and wear quite as well as paint.

The rustic form of seat at Fig. 2 can be constructed with round poles about 1½ in. to 2 in. diameter, with or without the bark. The latter is generally preferable as in time barked poles will start to peel, and very soon the whole of the bark will have disappeared.

The length of the poles as shown in the enlarged end view at Fig. 5, should be about 4 ft., this will allow of about 12 in. to be driven in the ground.

The supporting piece or strut B should be about
3 ft. 6 in. both of these pieces are pointed at the
ends and the strut should be shaped at the top to
fit into a notch cut in the back of the piece A.

The front leg of the seat, C, should be about
2 ft. 6 in. long, the end is sharpened and the seat
rail, D, notched in as at Fig. 6. The seat rail
can be of 4 in. by 2 in. wood, or it can be formed by
sawing down some round wood of larger diameter,
about 6 in. or so.

The seat and back strips should be either $1\frac{1}{4}$ in.
or $1\frac{1}{2}$ in. thick, depending on the length of the seat,
the width should be from 3 in. to 4 in. and they
should be nailed very securely. All the joints
can be marked out and cut before the lengths are
driven in the ground, or the seat can be made up
entirely and let into the ground into prepared
holes, the use of the material suggested however,
enables the work of jointing up the pieces to be
done when they are in position. Varnish is the
best finish for rustic work of this kind.

A GARDEN LINE REEL.

The reel shown at Fig. 1 will be found of great
use in the garden and is easily made from $\frac{1}{2}$ in.
wood with some 1 in. round (broomstick will be
found convenient). The section at Fig. 2 indicates
the method of construction, dimensions being fixed
to suit, a suitable size for the top piece A would be
8 in. by $1\frac{1}{8}$ in. by $\frac{1}{2}$ in. The lower piece B should
be about $1\frac{1}{2}$ in. wide, the middle piece may be
about 15 in. long and the inner piece C about $6\frac{1}{2}$ in.,

this allows of $\frac{1}{4}$ in. tenons which fit in holes bored in A and B.

The screw through the top piece A should fit loosely so that the top portion can revolve freely

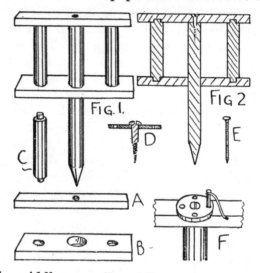

FIG. 1.   FIG 2

on the middle peg.   By adding a thin metal plate soldered to the screw as at D and drilled with four holes near the circumference, the reel can be fixed with a pin E as shown at F.

A SIMPLE LATCH.

Latches for garden gates and other purposes can be made from bar iron or steel, a suitable size being $\frac{3}{4}$ in. by $\frac{3}{16}$ in. or $\frac{1}{8}$ in.   A simple design is given at Fig. 1 with a section showing the method of securing the catch at Fig. 2 and a section through the centre of latch at Fig. 3.   All the parts can be cut out of a short length of bar as at A, B, C, D, E and F, which correspond with similar markings at Figs. 1 and 2. All the work can be done with file

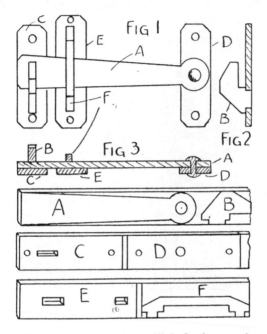

and drills, but a hacksaw will help in cutting out the shapes, and save time. The dimensions depend on the size required, the proportions given will be found suitable for a latch 4 in. long.

A HANGING FERN BASKET.

The fern basket shown at Fig. 1 is very easily made and forms a most effective method of growing many kinds of ferns and flowers. The material can be picked up in the neighbourhood of a wood. with the exception of the base which should be of planed wood about 10 in. square.

If the basket is to be placed in such a position that the bottom surface is shown, short lengths of bark covered branches can be split and attached

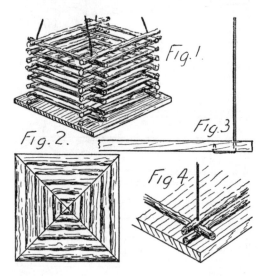

Fig. 1.

Fig. 2.

Fig. 3

Fig 4

to form a pattern as at Fig. 2. If this form of decoration is carried out, the four side wires should be fitted in position beforehand as at Fig. 3. It will be seen that the length of wire is passed through the bottom and the end is bent over twice at right angles, the point formed with a file and then driven into the wood. The wire should be long enough to be fastened to a ring at the top, but if desired the four pieces can be a little longer than the sides of the basket and either small chain or picture wire used to hold it up.   The round lengths of wood used for the sides should be the same length as the sides of the base, and each one should be drilled with a hole so that it can pass through the wire as at Fig. 4.

A coat of size should be applied to the finished work and then about two coats of varnish; this is not absolutely necessary, but owing to the necessity of using water, the coat of varnish will preserve the wood and make the basket last much longer. Large baskets to rest on the ground and made of much stouter material are very effective and no more difficult to make.

BIRD HOUSES.

All lovers of Nature are fond of birds and like to have them close at hand for observation or company, therefore simple little constructions similar to those shown at Fig. 1 will be welcomed.

The house at A is formed from a trunk of a tree sawn off to a slope at the top and hollowed out as at B ; this can be done with a red-hot iron or with gouges.   The top is nailed on and suitable fastenings placed at the back.   The house at C is made to a convenient size from wood about $\frac{3}{4}$ in. thick and provided with two compartments, the parts can be nailed together.   A simple house is shown in detail at D, it is better to use thick wood and give plenty of overhang to the roof.   Suitable inside dimensions would be 8 in. by 4 in. floor space, and 3 in. up to the eaves.   The bottom should project about $2\frac{1}{2}$ in. in front.

The wood will last much longer if it is creosoted or coated with one of the many wood preservatives on the market, but if this is done the house should

be left some time before being used, to allow the preservative to dry.

Bird houses should be placed in a shady spot against a tree or supported on a pole, it is not advisable to hang them against a wall. An interesting construction is a bird table, this can be made in the form of a circular piece of wood about

12 in. to 15 in. diameter, supported on a post about 3 ft. high. A shallow vessel should be provided for water and a shelter can be fitted over if desired. One method of forming the table is to saw off the end of a barrel, nail it to a post and to fill the space with sand. Birds will soon find out the sand and will enjoy sand baths, especially during the hot weather.

EASILY MADE FLOWER STANDS.

When flower time approaches many boys will be looking out for suitable designs for boxes and stands for growing flowers. Window boxes are not difficult to make, and provided they are strong enough, a plain nailed box is generally sufficient, but craftsmanship can be imparted to simple objects of this kind. The flower box shown at Fig. 1 is not intended, however, for the outside window sill, but it can be used on the inside or on a table or shelf, and although it can be used without a zinc lining, it is better to fit one if the expense is not a drawback. Suitable dimensions are given in the details of the parts, and these can be taken as a general indication of proportions. It will be seen that two methods of attaching the ends are shown, one is to let the long sides and the bottom into the shaped ends and to fit in a plain piece as at A for extra strength ; the other is to make the box with butt joints and either screw or nail the ends on. The former is the better method. If the box is not provided with a lining, the inside should be coated with pitch, this is melted and painted on thickly.

The upright stand shown in front elevation and sectional at Fig. 2 is quite easily made, but it uses up a fair amount of wood. It will be seen that the front and back pieces are shaped from a 42 in. by 15 in. by $\frac{3}{4}$ in. piece ; these are joined at the top

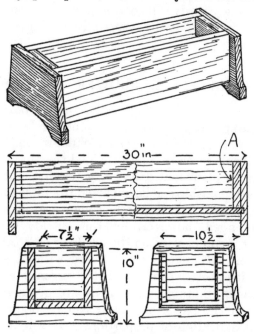

FIG. I

with two 10 in. by 9 in. by $\frac{3}{4}$ in. pieces and at the bottom with two 18 in. by 6 in. by $\frac{3}{4}$ in. pieces. Details of the dovetail joints at the top and the halving joints at the bottom are shown in the illustration.

The best method of construction is to prepare the shaped sides and to avoid gluing two lengths together, one of the wider timbers such as white-wood, satin walnut or hazel pine should be used. The opening should be marked out and sawn out with a bow saw and finished as neatly as possible. The bottom of the plant holder should be housed

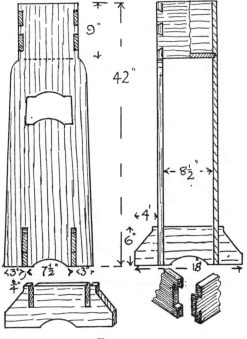

Fig. 2

into the sides, and the dovetails cut on the sides so that they can be marked on the edges of the front and back pieces. It is not usual to dovetail work in this way as the grain runs in opposite directions, but it is unavoidable.

Linings for the flower stands should be made

from thin sheet zinc, tinned sheet is not so suitable, although it can be used if it is thoroughly well coated with paint both inside and out. The metal should be securely soldered at all the joints ; it is better to use a large sheet and bend up the sides, but as this means waste in respect of the corner pieces which have to be cut out, it is more economical, if more laborious, to use separate pieces. This is more pronounced in large boxes than in the comparatively small stand at Fig. 2.

A TENT FOR CAMPING.

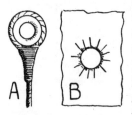

The tent shown at Fig. 1 is easily and cheaply made and can be carried on a cycle. The plan and elevation at Figs. 2 and 3 give the main dimensions and Fig. 4 illustrates the method of attaching the ridge and guy ropes. The two poles should be 5 ft. 6 in. long and $1\frac{1}{8}$ in. diameter, these can be in two pieces and fitted with a brass ferrule similar to a fishing rod. The ends should be fitted with short lengths of brass tube and long wire nails driven in, the heads being filed off to form projections. The ropes should be provided with thimbles with the rope bound round with string, or spliced as at diagram A. The guy ropes are fitted with toggles as at Fig. 5 and pegs

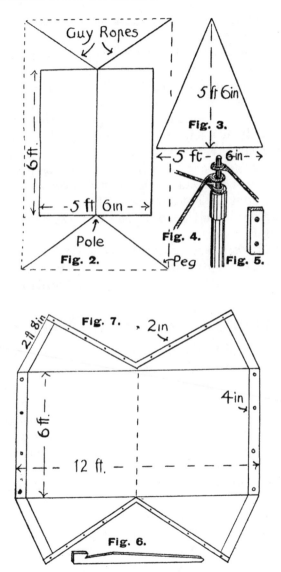

Guy Ropes

5 ft 6in

Fig. 3.

←— 5 ft ——6 in—→

6 ft.

←— 5 ft 6in —→

Pole

Fig. 2.

Peg

Fig. 4.

Fig. 5.

Fig. 7.

2 ft 8 in

2 in

4 in

6 ft.

←——— 12 ft. ———→

Fig. 6.

are provided as at Fig. 6; beech is suitable wood for these fittings.

The tent cloth at Fig. 7 can be of canvas or calico, the latter material is cheap and light and quite satisfactory in use. If the full width of 6 ft. can be obtained it will save a centre join. The end hems are 4 in. wide and the flaps must be cut out separately and joined on, the outside edges having 2-in. hems. Eyelet holes are worked at the ends of the ridge, along the bottom and on the flaps, as at diagram B, metal eyelets can be purchased, but it will do if the holes are cut out and bound round with stout linen thread in the same way as button-holing is done.

Cord loops are provided along the bottom for pegging the sides down, and long loops for threading inside one another are attached to the flaps.

COLLECTING GEOLOGICAL SPECIMENS.

For those boys who love the open air and who are keen on making collections, there is no more interesting study than Geology. It is surprising how much pleasure can be got from a day spent in a quarry or clay pit; it is equally surprising to learn what treasures can be found in these places. The quick eyes of the average boy can detect fossils and minerals which the casual observer fails to notice. An acquaintance of mine passed daily, for many years, a rock face which was crowded with fossils and was astonished when these were pointed out to him. Now, there are very few localities in England where a boy cannot find some quarry or pit or shore section, in clay, limestone, shale, etc., where fossils are waiting the advent of his hammer, and the equipment required is very simple.

First, a good hammer with a steel head is needed. A cast iron head is useless and is bound to break. A good nail hammer can be used but it is better to

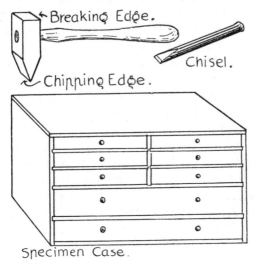

← Breaking Edge.

Chisel.

← Chipping Edge.

Specimen Case.

obtain one made for the purpose. A small cold chisel is essential to chip round the edges of a specimen embedded in hard rock or to trim up rough pieces. Make a point of taking away only small pieces of rocks and minerals, just large enough to be handled easily. Larger pieces are a burden to carry, and difficult to store.

A few localities, where fossils and minerals are found may be mentioned. Those who do not live near these places may visit some during the holidays.

Anyone living in the chalk area of S.E. England should have no difficulty in finding a chalk pit, where fossils are usually to be found. The clay beds below the chalk are often worked for material for bricks and these pits are happy hunting grounds for the geologist. The shores of the Isle of Wight are specially suitable for our purpose. From Alum Bay, around the South Coast, to Bembridge, one can scarcely go wrong.

The middle rocks of our English system are exposed from the coast of Dorset, across the country to the coast of Yorkshire. Either of these coasts should prove very profitable grounds for the fossil hunter.

The older rocks of Wales and the North of England have their special attractions. Many fossils can be found in the limestone and shales and in addition, beautiful crystals and minerals are to be found in almost any mine " tip." Of course, those who live near the coal fields should not fail to examine the waste heaps. Beautiful specimens of plants of the coal measures can be found in the shales which are thrown out of the pits. One can only give very general descriptions in a short article such as this. Local guide books are often useful aids in this matter, and the " Memoirs " of the Geological Survey can usually be purchased locally, and they give most useful information.

A haversack is the best thing to use for carrying the hammer, etc., and specimens. Take several pieces of newspaper and wrap up each specimen after making a note on the paper of any particulars of locality, etc. The hammer head has a knack of bumping against specimens not wrapped up and many a good fossil has been quite ruined on the homeward journey, through the lack of a piece of newspaper. Small specimens are easily carried in match boxes filled with cotton wool.

For storing the collection at home there is nothing better than a small nest of drawers with a place for label on the front of each drawer. These can be made quite easily by the average boy. The writer has a large one made from an old book shelf and a number of soap boxes cut down to make drawers. A bit of beading, a knob and plenty of staining, and the result is quite pleasing.

To obtain the names of specimens found, a visit should be paid to the local museum (if any). Helpful books for the young student are : " A First Book of Geology "—Wilmore : Macmillans ; " The Earth Shown to the Children " : Hawks.

A very good elementary text book and one containing much useful information is " Macmillans Elementary Geology," by Watts.

PUTTING IN A NEW PANE OF GLASS.

The first thing to do is to remove all the broken glass and cut away all the old putty as at 1. If the glass has been in position for a long time, the putty will be quite hard and it will probably be necessary to use an old knife and a hammer. Care must be taken in cleaning the putty behind the glass to avoid cutting into the wood. Generally the old putty will come away in small pieces and leave a clean space behind. The inside of the rebate should be scraped to the wood and then coated with paint. Measure up the size carefully and provide a new piece of glass measuring $\frac{1}{8}$ in. less each way than the size of the opening. The inside of the rebate should be coated with putty as at 2, the putty should be

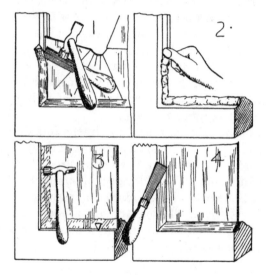

worked as soft as possible and the layer placed evenly. The next stage shown at 3 consists in placing the new piece of glass in position and pressing it down very carefully on the putty bed. Spread the fingers widely apart so that the pressure is evenly distributed. The glass can be kept in position with brads or with small triangular pieces of zinc as shown. The final stage is to press an even layer of putty in to the rebate and to smooth it down as at 4. Press the side of the knife at the required angle and work from top to bottom and side to side.

PROTECTING WATER PIPES FROM FROST.

The handy boy should be prepared to do all sorts of odd jobs at home, and at the approach of winter the water pipes should be fully protected from frost. If possible, during severe frosts at least, the water should be turned off at the main so as to free them from water, but where this is not practicable, the usual method is to wrap twisted strands of straw closely round the pipes. The straw should be picked out in long lengths and twisted into a thick rope. An outer covering of strips of thick felt or even sacking should be wrapped over the straw; a felt or sacking covering alone is not sufficient protection. The straw allows for a cushion of air between the frost and the pipe.

MAKING WHITELEAD PAINT.

This is the name given to a carbonate of lead produced by various processes and used for making paint. White lead is purchased in the form of paste and to make it into paint, it is necessary to add raw linseed oil and linseed oil or patent driers. To prepare the paint, the white lead should be beaten thoroughly to remove any water that may have been used to cover it, add to 6 lb. of the white lead 5 oz. of paste, or 5 tablespoons full of liquid, driers and thoroughly mix. The thick paste is now thinned down with linseed oil. It is usual to add a little red lead to the paint used for the first coat in order to assist the paint to dry.

RENEWING BROKEN SASH CORD.

Windows containing frames that move up and down by means of a weighted cord are called sashes, the cords are liable to break through constant wear, with the result that the weight falls down, the

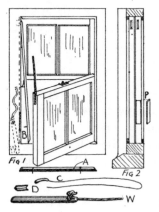

Fig 1

Fig 2

lower sash can be lifted only with difficulty, owing to the absence of the compensating weight and the top sash will fall to the bottom of the frame.

The method of dealing with a broken cord in lower sash is shown at Fig. 1, and consists in removing the sash from the frame and securing a new length of cord. To remove the sash, it is necessary to take out the bottom bead as at A, this is done by inserting an old wide chisel or a screwdriver under the bead close to the nails, raise the wood sufficiently to bring the heads of the nails above the bead when let down flat again, and then withdraw the nails with a pair of pincers. The side bead, B, can then be lifted off quite easily. Some advise taking the side bead off first, but unless great care is used, the entry mark of the chisel shows up very plainly.

The next step is to lift the sash out, pull out the broken length and then to remove the weight from the side of the frame. On examining the framing, a pocket piece P, as at Fig. 2, will be seen; drive a gimlet in this piece, hammer slightly on the outside and then pull out. The weight with remainder of cord can now be pulled out. Next measure off the new length and pass it over the pulley to the inside, this is done with a " mouse," a length of string having a piece of lead at one end as at C, made by hammering over a bent piece of lead as at D. The mouse is slipped over the pulley, after tying the free end of the string to one end of the cord. The cord is now tied to the weight as at W, and the latter replaced. The outside end of cord is fastened to the frame with two nails, taking care that the length is correct. Replace sash, drive back the nails in the beading and then replace. With an upper sash, remove the front sash first and place on a chair, then pull out the inner bead so that the top sash will come forward. The same procedure is then followed.

THE ART OF SOLDERING.

Many boys have tried to do small soldering jobs and failed mainly because they have not appreciated the necessity of the first essential of successful soldering, that of cleanliness. Solder will run only on a perfectly bright metal surface coated with a flux. The air acts very quickly on all metals and forms a film of oxide on which solder will not flow; it is therefore most important that the portion of

the metal to be soldered must be scraped bright.
It is also important to have a good copper bit, or
soldering iron as it is called. The piece of copper
should be rectangular and about $\frac{1}{2}$ in. square in
section, and weigh $\frac{1}{2}$ lb. or so, it should be rivetted
to an iron shaft attached to a large wooden handle.
It is only asking for trouble to attempt to do good
work with a bit weighing an ounce or so, the piece
of copper must be heavy enough to retain heat for
some time.

It is necessary to have some flux, this is used in
the form of a liquid or a paste, to spread on the
work before soldering to enable the solder to flow
over the prepared surface. The commonest form
of flux is killed spirits made by placing small
pieces of zinc in a stone jar half filled with spirits
of salts, known also as hydrochloric acid. As
this liquid is poisonous and liable to damage the
clothes, the more convenient paste flux is advised.
Several preparations are available and obtainable
in shallow tins, they are cleanly in use and quite
effective. A length or two of ordinary tinman's
solder, an old pocket knife, a worn flat file or two
will complete the equipment.

For the sake of example we will suppose we
have a small kettle to mend. First of all the metal
surrounding the leaky places should be thoroughly
cleaned, this does not mean washing, even with
hot soda and water, but actual scraping in order
to obtain a perfectly bright surface. This may be
done with a knife or file, but the surface must be
thoroughly scraped. The flux should be spread over
the cleaned portion, a good method is to bruise the

end of a length of cane and use it as a brush. The coating of flux will prevent the air tarnishing the bright surface as it is important to keep it bright.

In the meantime the soldering bit should be placed over a gas ring until it becomes quite hot but not red-hot. The heating will cause the copper to become dull and it is as necessary to have the bit bright as well as the metal which has to be soldered, a worn file should be used to take off the scale and expose the pure metal underneath. The heated bit should now be dipped into the flux and then touched with the solder. If the heat is right the solder will run over the parts which have been coated with flux. Too high a temperature will cause the flux to generate a lot of steam, a slight sizzle should be heard and a a little vapour should be seen. If on the first touch on the flux, the bit proves to be too hot, a wait of a minute or so will be sufficient to lower the temperature. This method of applying the solder to the end of the bit is called tinning.

We are now ready for actual soldering and if the article is held, say between the knees or in a vice, and the point of the bit placed in the centre of the cleaned portion, the solder from the bit will run over the surface when it has become hot enough. If there is insufficient solder on the end of the bit, the stick of solder should be placed at the point of intersection of bit and surface and sufficient will melt and run in with the rest. At first the bit may cool off too quickly, especially if the copper end is small, but when reheated cleaned and tinned, again the job may be finished.

A hole in the bottom of the kettle cannot be covered with a lump of solder, it must be patched with a small piece of tinned sheet. The surface surrounding the hole should be scraped for about ½ in. all round and it is more than probable that the hole will be enlarged, but this does not matter much. A circular piece of tinned sheet, cut from an old can, should be fitted over the hole with a good margin of overlap, and both sides should be scraped bright. Both the surface surrounding the hole and the patch should be coated with flux and then coated with solder, otherwise tinned. The thinnest possible layer of solder is required but it must entirely cover the surface. Now place the patch in position and press it down with the heated bit, hold it there until the solder runs and the job is done.

All other soldering jobs are done in more or less the same way, and with a little practice, it will be possible to become quite adept in the use of the soldering iron.

WHITEWASH AND DISTEMPERING.

There is little, if any, difference in the method of applying whitewash or distemper, but there is a difference in the materials themselves. When considering the coating of walls and ceilings, something should be known about the particular properties of the materials that are in general use and their fitness for the work in view. Whitewash is the name given to a mixture of whiting and size, and is generally used for ceilings. Limewash, often miscalled whitewash, is a mixture of slaked lime and water, and is used for the walls and ceilings of outhouses, sheds, poultry houses, etc. Distemper is a water paint obtainable in a large variety of colourings, including white, and is generally washable.

The use of limewash is general for all kinds of sheds and buildings where animals and birds are housed, and in places where the conditions call for highly sanitary treatment. It is advisable to prepare the surfaces by washing them with strong soda water in which a little soft soap has been dissolved ; in positions where special sanitary precautions are needed, the surface should be sprayed with a strong solution of disinfectant, such as carbolic acid, in the proportion of one part of the acid to thirty-five parts of water. The limewash is prepared by placing a sufficient quantity of quicklime into an old tub, tank, or waterproof box, and then covering it with boiling water. When the lime has dissolved and crumbled to a powder, add more water to produce a liquid of a creamy consistency. The wash should be applied to a dry surface with a fairly stiff brush, but owing to the nature of the material, an old, or at least a cheap fibre, brush should be used, kept for the purpose and not used for anything else.

The limewash should be rubbed into the surface with considerable vigour, allowing for a fairly thick coating. A little sulphate of zinc and common salt, in the proportion of 1 lb. of each to a bushel of lime, dissolved in the mixing water will make the wash harden as it dries. Size should not be used with limewash as it spoils its disinfecting quality, but for interior work, the addition of boiled linseed oil, in the proportion of $\frac{1}{2}$ pint of oil to a bushel of lime, will help the wash to bind and prevent it rubbing off easily.

When using limewash, the clothes should be covered with an overall and the hair covered with a cap. After several coats of limewash have been applied to a surface, it will begin to fall off in flakes; when this occurs, the surface should be scraped and rewashed.

Whitewash is more generally used for ceilings and it is made by breaking up some balls of whiting, placing them in a perfectly clean pail and covering with clean water. When the material has dissolved, pour off the surplus water and thoroughly mix up the resultant paste. While the whiting is dissolving, heat up some double size and then pour it into the paste, together with a small quantity of powdered blue and mix up well. The usual proportions are three pounds of whiting to one pint of size. The mixture will form a jelly when cold, and this is mixed with cold water to a creamy consistency just before it is to be used. When using whitewash, the surface should be washed over with clean water, using a worn whitewash brush; if the walls of the room are papered, sheets of newspaper should be pinned close up to the ceiling to prevent splashes.

Do not apply whitewash until the surface to which it is to be applied is quite dry, and make quite sure that the surface is perfectly clean. It is never satisfactory to apply clean whitewash to a dirty surface. It is advisable to do the work with the windows closed, this will prevent unequal drying. The liquid should be kept well stirred while it is being used to prevent the formation of a sediment, the brush should be immersed fully in the pail, and the tip stroked on the edge or on a stout wire stretched across the pail from side to side. The brush should be applied to the ceiling with a slapping motion, drawn along to the length of a stroke and then brought back again with a similar action. This method will empty the brush and give an even coating. At first there will be a tendency to splash, but after a few strokes, the method will become easier and the coatings even. Ceilings that have become blackened or stained may not work clean when washed ; it will be necessary to apply a coating of thin plaster made by adding sufficient plaster of Paris to a pail of water to form a creamy liquid. The same material formed into a paste can be used to fill up cracks, apply with a clean knife and leave the surface quite smooth. Any mixture made with plaster of Paris, should be used as quickly as possible after being made, it sets very quickly and soon becomes useless.

Although coloured distempers can be made by adding finely ground powder colours to a whitewash mixture, it is better to purchase a well-known brand and mix it according to the directions supplied by the manufacturer. Distemper is applied more in the method followed in painting than in whitewashing, in so far as the brush is concerned ; the best form of brush being that known as a one-knot distemper brush, made of pure bristles. Bristles are somewhat expensive, but with care will last a lifetime. The distemper should be thoroughly worked into the surface with the strokes of the brush horizontal; it may be necessary in places to use the brush with a vertical motion, but although it is not so important to have a regularity of brush strokes as in painting, it is better to work with some uniformity.

Light colours look best when they are applied to a white surface, and when using brilliant colours, great care must be taken to see that there are no stains on the wall, and to keep the distemper well stirred. Walls and ceilings that have not been distempered or whitewashed before should be coated with clearcole to prevent the too rapid absorption of the distemper. Clearcole is prepared by boiling up a pailful of size and then pouring the hot size into another pail containing a quart of soaked whiting. The mixture is applied hot and acts as a priming, but care must be taken to apply the brush rapidly in all directions in order to keep a wet edge going all the time.

PAPERHANGING.

Although in this article it is not proposed to deal with the choice of wallpaper the boy who is going to do paperhanging should know something about the various kinds. The greater proportion of the papers used are machine printed with colours and designs suitable for all types and sizes of rooms. The price depends more on the substance or thickness of the paper than on the design which is printed on it, and as a rule it is more difficult to hang a cheap thin paper or an expensive thick paper than one of medium thickness and of a medium price. The modern tendency is towards a plain paper with no pattern, but a popular wallpaper is that known as a sanitary washable paper and which is printed in oil or distemper colours. The expensive papers include those with raised and embossed designs, satin and glazed finishes and patterns containing gold.

It is usual in estimating the quantity of paper required to allow one piece in seven for waste in trimming and matching the pattern, in plain papers, however, there is very little waste. The easiest way of ascertaining the number of rolls or pieces of paper for a room, is to measure the total length of the walls, ignoring windows and doors, multiply this measurement by the height and divide by the area of one piece of paper. The length of a piece of wallpaper is 12 yds. and the width 21 in., so that the area can be taken roughly as 60 sq. ft. For example, a room measuring 12 ft. by 12 ft. by 8 ft. would take seven pieces, allowing for waste.

Having provided the paper, the next step is to trim the edges with a large pair of scissors. This is a long job, requiring careful cutting, and it is worth while, considering the small extra charge involved, to get the dealer to cut off the edges on a trimming machine. If the cutting is to be done at home, the best way is to sit down with the feet extended, rest the roll of paper on them, take up one end and trim the edge with the scissors in one hand, while the other winds up the roll.

It is rarely satisfactory to paste new paper on the top of old, the walls should therefore be stripped and cleaned ; this is done by wetting the paper with a large sponge and peeling it off. One strip should be taken at a time, working from the bottom upwards. If the paper gets thoroughly wet, it will pull away quite easily, but it may be necessary to use a stripping knife to assist it in places ; a fairly pliable table knife can be used, but care should be taken to prevent it digging into the plaster.

The next thing is to prepare the paste by putting about 4 lb. of flour in a clean pail and mix it up thoroughly with sufficient water to form a stiff batter quite free from lumps. Add about 1 oz. of powdered alum and stir in boiling water until the paste thickens. Leave it to get cold before it is used. Some builders' merchants keep ready-made paste, or it can be obtained in powder form ready for mixing with water, but the home made paste will be found very satisfactory.

The next step is to cut the paper into lengths, but special attention must be paid to the pattern ; if it is a bold one, the whole of it should appear on the top. Allow a surplus of 3 in. or 4 in., and place the lengths, after matching the pattern, one on top of the other on a long table or some boards supported on trestles or boxes at a suitable height.

The work of paperhanging should be commenced at one of the angles of the room, preferably by the chimney breast, farthest away from the light.

The back of the paper is now covered with paste, beginning from the bottom of the paper and working away from the centre to the outsides, taking care that it is entirely covered with an even coating of paste. When the required length is pasted, fold the bottom of the paper over so that the two pasted surfaces are together, draw up the remainder, cover with paste and cover over as before.

The pasted paper is now placed on the arm, and from a convenient position on a pair of steps, allow the paper to unfold and hang down straight and then place the top in position on the wall. The edge can be trued with a plumbline if necessary, but it is usual to work with the eye. The paper, when hanging down straight, can be smoothed with a soft brush, a clean broom-head, is quite useful for this purpose ; the surplus top and bottom can be cut off with the scissors, the usual method of marking being to draw the point of the scissors along the angle made by the wall and ceiling or picture rail, and the wall and the skirting board. The paper is now finally smoothed down.

The next and following lengths are pasted in the same way, but care must be taken when hanging them to see that the pattern matches exactly and the edges meet. It does not do to depend on the first pattern below the eye, the next two or three connecting points should be noticed, and any adjustments made before the paper is finally attached to the wall. It is useful to have a flannel covered roller for running over the joins, but if the brush is carefully used, and where necessary, the paper is stroked lightly, using a dry cloth, there will be no difficulty in getting the paper to adhere closely to the wall. The joins on wall paper should be arranged as far as possible to face the light from the windows ; with a thin paper this does not matter very much. With fairly thick papers, the join is noticeable and for this reason it is usual to trim both edges so that they fit together without any overlap. If thick paper is used, it should be machine-trimmed to ensure a perfectly straight edge.

When embossed papers are used, ordinary paste is hardly strong enough and it is advisable to add glue to the paste, but it will be necessary to use the paste hot. It is not an easy matter to keep a large quantity of paste hot, but if it is placed in a bowl and the bowl rested on top of a pail filled with hot water, renewed from time to time, the main difficulty will be solved.

STAINS AND STAINING.

Staining lends itself to many treatments, from the darkening of floor boards to the decorative colouring of wood, either as an ornamental feature in itself, or as a means of imitating the colouring of an expensive wood on a light or inferior wood. It can be considered as an alternative to painting, but while paint obscures the original appearance of the wood, stain enables its natural beauty to be preserved. Stained wood can be finished by polishing or varnishing, the latter giving as sanitary and durable a surface as paint ; but to obtain the best effect, it is important to prepare a perfectly smooth surface with glasspaper and to leave it quite clean.

There are four kinds of stain in ordinary use, these are known as water, oil, spirit and chemical stains ; they are all more or less transparent and can be finished with polish or varnish. In addition, oil and spirit varnish stains are prepared for direct application. Some of the varnish stains are sufficiently opaque to be used on previously stained, varnished or polished surfaces, such as articles of furniture.

Water stains are formed by colour soluble in water and are of a transparent nature. Those in general use are vandyke brown, raw sienna, burnt sienna, raw umber, burnt umber and mahogany lake, this selection covers a range of browns and reds ; blue-black and indigo supply blues, yellow lake and gamboge form good yellows, a good green is found in terre vert and a black in logwood. Many aniline dyes are suitable and supply a large range of intermediate colourings. Water stains are inexpensive and suitable for many purposes, but they have a tendency to swell the grain of the wood. To prevent the grain rising up under the action of the stain, the wood should be damped with clean water, allowed to dry and then rubbed with glasspaper to a smooth surface. Water stains can be mixed with a weak size solution when applied to wood of a porous nature, but as a rule it is better to apply it pure and not too strong. If a deep shade of the colour is required, two or more applications are preferable to one deep stain which is apt to show uneven patches when dry.

Water staining must not be confused with water coating in which the body colour, and not the transparent colour, is mixed with size and applied to the wood. In this method of staining, the natural grain of the wood is hidden, but it is useful when large surfaces have to be coloured quickly in a manner similar to that employed in distempering ; it should not be used for good work.

Spirit stains are composed mainly of aniline dyes and pigments easily dissolved in spirit or naphtha ; they are obtainable in liquid form, or as powder to be dissolved in methylated spirit. They are more expensive than water stains, and as they dry very quickly are more difficult to apply, but a great variety of most brilliant colourings are available. The stain should be applied freely and evenly, but the edges of the stain should not be permitted to dry until the whole of the surface has been covered. If this is not attended to, it will be difficult to avoid lines of a deeper colour at places where the wet stain has joined a dry portion. The staining should be done across the narrow portion of the work, beginning at the top and a pool of liquid stain should be kept on the move until the whole of the surface is covered.

Oil stains are made with the same pigments as used in water stains, but the vehicle is composed of 1 part of linseed oil, 2 parts turpentine and $\frac{1}{2}$ a part of liquid driers, the only difference in the colours being that they are ground in oil instead of water. The stain is easily applied and it penetrates deeply into the wood ; it requires a day or two to dry, but it takes any kind of finish. It is admirably adapted for amateur use particularly on porous wood. With hard woods a little more turpentine can be used and for very porous woods, the proportion of oil can be increased slightly.

Chemical stains are generally colourless liquids which change the colour of the wood to which they are applied; ammonia and iron sulphate are examples of liquids capable of darkening wood, and the fumes of ammonia are utilised for darkening, oak. Permanganate of potash is another example of a chemical stain, the crystals are dissolved in water and the liquid will impart a rich reddish-brown stain. As a rule, chemical stains are not so permanent as liquid stains and are not used to any great extent.

Oil varnish stains are more simple to apply than varnish stains made with spirit, the latter are more or less opaque and can be used on all kinds of polished furniture or even on painted surfaces. It is not advisable to apply them direct to new wood; the latter should be stained and sized first. Old furniture made of stained wood can be renovated quite easily by using a suitable colour in an oil varnish stain.

Wax stains are easily made by adding powder colours to a mixture of beeswax and turpentine; wax is a good polish for hardwoods, especially oak, and it can be used on top of an oil or water stain to obtain a deeper colour; it will also impart a rich effect to the surface. A wax stain is useful for improving the colour of any kind of polished surface and it can be used with good effect on linoleum or stained floor boards.

Floor boards should be stained with oil stain and then wax polished or varnished; permanganate of potash can be used, but it is not so effective as an oil stain. For a quick drying brown stain similar in colour to dark walnut and giving an egg shell finish, ordinary black stove enamel diluted with turpentine is very effective.

Stain should be applied with a ready ground or worn-in hog hair brush, either oval or flat in shape. As far as possible staining brushes should be kept for use with one colour, but if several stains are to be applied with the same brush, the greatest care should be taken to clean them thoroughly. Spirit stains will usually give way if allowed to soak in methylated spirit and then washed in hot water in which soda has been dissolved. Oil and water stain brushes can generally be sufficiently cleaned with soda water and soft soap.

ENAMELLING AND VARNISHING.

In many ways these two methods of finishing a surface are similar, mainly because they both produce a glossy surface, although enamels are obtainable which impart a matt or semi-glossy surface. Enamel is a high-grade paint made for use on either wood or metal, and it can be obtained in many colours. In enamelling particularly, the preparation of the surface is of first importance, and unless a good body of undercoating of suitable paint is applied, the finish will not be entirely satisfactory.

To deal first with the enamelling of new wood surfaces, the wood must be finished quite smooth with glasspaper, and a coating of stopping or shellac applied in order to fill up the pores of the wood. This is rubbed down smooth and followed by a couple of coats of paint, each one being rubbed down before the next is applied. For this purpose, glasspaper can be used, but the finest surface is obtained by using pumice powder, the method being to dust the powder on to a small piece of thick felt made slightly damp. Rub the pad with a circular motion, renewing the powder from time to time, and when the surface feels quite smooth, wipe it with a clean cloth to remove all dust and then proceed with the next coat. Care must be taken to see that the paint is quite dry before it is rubbed down. There are many proprietary enamels on the market and manufacturers usually supply a suitable paint for the undercoating ; this should not be applied to new wood until at least one coat of ordinary paint has been applied and rubbed down smooth.

To enamel existing paint work, either in the form of furniture or on walls, first wash it with strong soda water, rinse with clean water and then rub it down. All cracks and holes should be filled up, and for this purpose obtain some finely ground whiting or plaster of Paris, mix it with gum to a thick cream and press it into the cracks with a stiff knife. When the stopping has dried quite hard, smooth it off and proceed with the undercoating.

The best brush to use is a flat bristle, bought ready ground or worn in by previous use with ordinary paint. The enamel should be stirred up thoroughly, every bit of the sediment at the bottom of the tin being incorporated, and it should not be allowed to settle until the work is finished. As enamel sets very much quicker than paint, any work begun should be finished at the one time, and to obtain the best effect, the work should be done in a warm dry room, free from dust. When enamelling the walls of a room, the windows should be kept closed until the enamel has set, and on no account should be work be done in a damp atmosphere or in a low temperature.

In applying enamel, the brush should be held as lightly as possible and used with a slight pressure only. As enamel naturally spreads in all directions and forms a smooth surface without marks, the use of a coarse or even a heavy pressure with a fine brush, will render the flow less effective. The surface should be covered evenly with light straight strokes of the brush, and every effort should be made to avoid having unequal quantities of enamel on the brush.

The above directions apply to the application of enamel on metal, but for this purpose special enamel is obtainable. It is equally important to prepare the surface and to give it a good undercoating well rubbed down. In enamelling a bath, special bath enamel and undercoating should be obtained, but it is most important that the previous enamel or paint should be cleaned off to remove all traces of grease. The directions supplied by the manufacturer should be followed carefully, and when the enamel is perfectly dry, the bath should be filled with cold water, the plug removed and hot water allowed to run in. In this way the cold water will give place very gradually to hot, and when filled entirely, the hot water should be allowed to stand until quite cold.

Varnish is another means of applying an enamelled surface, but instead of being coloured, it is transparent or translucent. There are two kinds of varnish, oil and spirit, but the former is more generally suitable for amateur use. Oil varnish is made in various grades for indoor and outdoor use and when purchasing, the purpose for which it is to be used should be stated. Like enamel, varnish should be applied with a worn-in bristle brush, preferably flat, and it should be perfectly clean.

The surface of new wood should be coated with size, the powder form being the most convenient, as it is easily dissolved in hot water. After the size has been applied and the surface is quite dry, it should be rubbed down with a damp felt pad and pumice powder. In order to save varnish and to give a hard surface, it is usual to apply two coats of size, each one being rubbed down when hard. If a second coat of varnish is applied, the first should be allowed to get quite hard before the final coat is applied. When varnish is applied to a previously painted surface, the paint should be washed down with strong soda water to remove grease and dirt, but it should be thoroughly rinsed in clean water and dried with a dry cloth.

The painted surface should be rubbed down with pumice powder and there should be no blemishes on the paint work if a perfect finish is required. Graining is usually finished with a coat of varnish, in this case, care must be taken in rubbing down ; the original coat of varnish should not be rubbed so much that none of it remains, all that is necessary is to remove any roughness felt on the surface.

PAINTING AND DECORATING.

Most boys at some time or other like to do painting, and should know something about the materials. As paint is used as a preservative as well as a decorative medium, some consideration must be given to the special kind of paint required. It is advisable to use always the best quality available ; the best paints are composed of a finely ground base and pigment mixed with superfine oils, with the result that a larger area of surface can be covered than is possible with a cheap paint which as a rule does not retain its colour and is not so durable. When purchasing paint, go to a reputable firm and state if it is for interior or exterior use ; as a rough guide for quantity, one lb. of good paint will cover about 30 sq. ft. on new wood and about 50 sq. ft. when applied on the top of old paint.

Three brushes are usually required, one with fairly soft bristles is used as a duster before the paint is applied, another, known as a sash tool, is used on narrow surfaces, and the third is a ground brush used for broad surfaces. Before being used for paint, the brushes should be soaked in hot water so that the bristles will tighten up and not work out in use. After use they should be very thoroughly cleaned, either with turpentine or with strong soda water and soap and then dried. If the brushes are likely to be used for the same colour within a short period, they may be suspended in turpentine, but the excess liquid should be pressed out before use by stroking the brush on the side of the receptacle.

The preparation of the surface for painting is generally of more importance than the actual application of the paint. In repainting interior work, the old surface should be thoroughly cleaned with soap and water or strong soda water ; it is not sufficient just to wipe the surface over, it should be scrubbed down with a brush in order to remove all grease and dirt, then thoroughly rinsed with clean water and left to dry.

In painting exterior work, much depends on the appearance of the old paint. If the work has been exposed to the heat of the sun and has become blistered, or has become old and brittle, it will be necessary to remove the entire surface; for this purpose it is usual to use a blow-lamp, burning vapourised paraffin. The flame is applied to the old paint, and when sufficiently soft, the paint can be scraped off with a steel scraper. When the surface is clean, rub it down with glasspaper, or a piece of thick felt, made damp and coated with pumice powder. The surface must be wiped quite clean and then coated with priming, followed by at least two coats of paint. In painting exterior iron or other metal work, it is usual to scrape off all the old paint ; this may be done with an old knife or file, but the most satisfactory method is to use a wire brush. Before a new coat of paint is applied to

ironwork, a coat of anti-rust priming should be
applied.

New woodwork, before being painted, should be
smoothed with glasspaper and a coat of patent
knotting applied over all knots. This should be
followed by a coat of priming rubbed well into the
wood ; it does not matter very much what kind of
paint is used for the priming so long as it will not
clash too much with the proper paint. The priming coat should be rubbed down when dry so that
a good surface is left. Usually two coats of paint are
applied after the priming, but for a lasting surface,
especially on exterior work, a third coat is advisable.

As far as possible, in applying paint, the strokes
of the brush should be in the same direction. In
painting a panelled door, the panels should be done
first, then the centre portions between the panels
known as the muntin, all covered with vertical
strokes. The cross rails are painted with horizontal
strokes, and the stiles, which are on the outside
and run from top to bottom, painted with vertical
strokes. It will be seen that the beginnings and
endings of the brush strokes on the inner portions
of the door are covered in turn and the result is an
evenly distributed series of marks.

It is a mistake to have too much paint on the
brush, keep the paint well stirred and make sure
that there is no sediment at the bottom of the tin.
After dipping the brush into the paint, stroke it
on the side of the pot to remove the surplus ; it is
a good plan to stretch a length of wire across the
top of the paint pot from side to side and use it to
wipe the brush on. In this way waste can be

prevented, as drops of paint are less liable to drop on the floor.

When the paint is on the surface, work it well by moving the brush from end to end, gradually decreasing the pressure until the last strokes are as light as possible. When working close to glass, wallpaper or any surface which is not to be painted, protect it with a sheet of zinc or piece of cardboard, the latter should be wiped from time to time to keep it quite clean.

When a job is finished, put the lid on the paint pot so that the contents are quite air-tight ; if a film is allowed to form on the surface of the paint, it will cause trouble when next the paint is used. When paint has been allowed to stand for a long time without being used, special attention should be paid to the surface. If a film should have been formed, remove it carefully before stirring up the paint.

As a rule there is no need to dilute paint either by the addition of linseed oil or turpentine, but for a priming coat, a little more turpentine can be added, and to impart a glossier surface, a little extra linseed oil can be added. It must be remembered that the more oil there is in the paint the longer it takes to dry, and with exterior paint ing a quick drying paint is an advantage, as it is not so liable to collect the dust.

POLISH AND POLISHING.

There are several kinds of polish, each requiring its own method of application. To enumerate them all would be impossible within the limits of this book, so that only those in common use will be described. French polish can be purchased ready for use, but it may be made by dissolving 3 ozs. of shellac in half pint of methylated spirit. Oil polish is merely raw or boiled linseed oil used without further preparation. Wax polish is composed of beeswax dissolved in turps or some similar medium. Convenient preparations ready for use in the form of prepared wax and floor or furniture polish are obtainable.

In all kinds of polishing, the first and often the most important operation is the preparation of the surface. The wood should be perfectly dry, the surface quite smooth and free from finger marks and any holes filled up with prepared stopping. A good stopping can be made with French chalk or finely powdered whiting mixed with gum. The grain of porous wood should be filled with a mixture of plaster of Paris and methylated spirit, and when dry, cleaned off with fine glasspaper or pumice powder applied with a thick felt pad.

French polishing is usually considered as beyond the capabilities of the amateur, but with ordinary care, small surfaces at least can be done without difficulty. The first thing to do is to provide a rubber ; this is made from washed linen rag of fine texture covering a pad formed from white sheet wadding. Remove the skin from the wadding and work it into a cone shape about 4 in. long and 3 in. diameter at the large end ; place it in the centre of the rag, which should be about 15 in. square, first soaking it with polish, then fold over on the small end, place the corners over in turn and twist the remainder to form a convenient rubber for holding in the fingers. The rubber is now rubbed over the surface in a circular motion so that the whole of the surface is covered; never allow the rubber to stand still, keep it continually on the move and make the polish go as far as possible.

A film of shellac will gradually form on the surface, this must be added to, but it is advisable to do the work in stages, allowing each layer of polish to harden for an hour or two before being touched again. At least half a dozen coats should be applied. If the rubber shows a tendency to stick, a touch of linseed oil will ease it, but this should be done very sparingly. When the surface bears a dull gloss, and the smoothness satisfactory, the final operation of spiriting off should be done.

Spiriting off consists of rubbing over the work with a pad made of wadding, saturated in methylated spirit, squeezed nearly dry and then wrapped in a clean linen rag, doubled over to give two thicknesses of material under the pad. The rubber is used lightly at first and then the pressure gradually increased as the spirit works out of the rubber. The action is to harden and burnish the surface and great care should be taken to use as little of the spirit as is consistent with the object in view. Many beginners spoil the work in the final stages by either allowing the rubber to stick on the surface or by using too much spirit.

Oil polishing is an admirable method for the amateur, its main advantages over French polishing are its simplicity and the fact that it does not show marks, but it takes time and considerable friction. To obtain a lasting effect, the polishing should be spread over a few weeks, each application of the oil being rubbed dry and left for a few days before the next is applied. A soft linen rag should be used as a rubber ; it should be dipped in raw or boiled linseed oil and applied to the surface so as to completely cover it. The rubber must be used continually until the surface is quite hard and dry ; it is hardly possible to polish the surface too much, but when it appears sufficiently glossy, a final rubbing should be done with a rubber soaked in spirit as in French polishing ; this is not essential, however. Oil polish is excellent as a treatment for oak, it does not give such a brilliant finish as shellac, but is in every way suitable for the amateur.

Wax polishing imparts an egg shell finish or matt surface and when used on hardwoods such as walnut or mahogany, gives the work a velvety appearance. The surface is not so hard or so durable as it would be if French or oil polished, but on the other hand it can be done very rapidly and is easily renovated. For white woods it is better to use white beeswax, but for ordinary work, the ordinary yellow variety will be good enough. The wax should be shredded as finely as possible, placed in an earthenware pot and covered with turpentine. If allowed to stand for several days and stirred from time to time, the wax will dissolve, but a quick method is to place the pot in a saucepan of hot water and allow it to simmer over a small gas ring. For soft woods the wax should be used as a thick paste, but for all hardwoods, it need not be more than of a creamy consistency. A piece of well washed flannel forms the best rubber, a good plan is to use strips of the material about 1 in. wide, wrap them round and round to form a circular pad which can be tied in the middle with string. The wax should be applied in thin coats and thoroughly well rubbed into the wood, the finishing should be done with a clean soft cloth. Wax polish can be kept quite soft if kept in an air-tight cannister, and it can be stained to any colour by using an oil stain.

PASTE AND GLUE.

There are many uses for paste in the house, among them being paper-hanging, bookbinding and book repairs, mounting scraps and photos, and the making of fancy articles in strawboard or cardboard, which are covered with paper or fabric. Paste and glue, together with gum, are the more commonly used forms of adhesive preparations, paste and gum are mainly used for paper and fabrics, while glue is used for wood. There are other forms of adhesives used for joining up various materials, but they are generally classified under cements.

Paste is usually made either with flour or starch ; as a rule it is mixed with water, but sometimes it is made with the addition of a gum to strengthen it. A good flour paste is made by mixing ordinary white or rye flour with water to form a stiff batter without lumps. It is thinned to the consistency of cream, and then boiling water is added slowly, while it is being stirred, until the paste thickens, when it is boiled for 5 minutes. A few drops of oil of cloves or carbolic acid can be added to the paste before it is used, in order to preserve it, but as all flour pastes are liable to become watery and lose their strength, it is usual to mix up sufficient for the work in hand and not to bother about its keeping qualities.

Starch paste is more expensive, but it has excellent sticking qualities, and when a few drops of oil of cloves is added when the paste is cold, it can be kept for a long time, particularly if it is stored in an air-tight bottle or jar. A good method of making the paste is to mix a tablespoonful of ordinary white starch with cold water until it forms a creamy liquid. Boiling water is now poured on to it slowly, stirring all the time, until it thickens and it becomes a translucent jelly. A spoonful of gum arabic is often added to the paste to strengthen it; this can be done while the paste is still hot, but the oil of cloves should not be added until it is cold.

Another method of making flour paste to give it greater tenacity, is to add Scotch glue or size after thickening. The method is to mix rye flour to a creamy consistency, add boiling water until the paste thickens, then pour in a quarter of its bulk of melted Scotch glue, or one-third of the bulk of melted concentrated size. The mixture should be boiled up and thoroughly stirred. To preserve it and prevent discolouration, melt $\frac{3}{4}$ oz. of alum in each quart of the mixing water. This paste can be used either hot or cold, but it works easier when hot, and is adapted for use in hanging thick and embossed wallpapers and also for fixing linoleum.

A strong and clean paste for mounting photographs can be made from dextrine, but considerable care is required in making it. One pint of water is placed in an enamelled double saucepan, placed over a gas flame and brought to a temperature of exactly 160° F. Next stir into the water very slowly 10 ozs. of white dextrine, but the temperature must not be allowed to alter and the stirring must be continued until it forms a perfectly clear solution ; 3 minims each of oil of cloves and oil of wintergreen are then added. When the solution has cooled, it should be poured into wide necked bottles or jars, covered with a cork, and allowed to stand undisturbed for about a fortnight. The paste will gradually congeal and become white, when it is ready for use. The paste should not be exposed to the air when not in use, otherwise it will harden and become useless.

Glue is available in several forms, when used in large quantities it is melted up with water from cakes, but for occasional use, the various forms of fish glue, usually packed in tube form, are more convenient. Of ordinary cake glues, Scotch is the strongest ; French glue is more transparent, but not so strong. Glue loses much of its strength by being repeatedly reheated, so it is advisable to make no more than is necessary for use at one time. The best way to make it is to break up a cake into small pieces, place it in the inner pot of an iron glue pot, cover it with water and leave it for a few hours to form a jelly. The glue is now brought to boiling point, the froth removed, and it is then used as hot as possible. It may be made in a jar placed in a saucepan.

In using glue, the best result is obtained by applying it to the wood after it has been warmed and in a warm room, apply with a bristle brush as rapidly as possible, and take care that the brush has been previously soaked in hot water to prevent the bristles working out. It is not necessary to apply a thick coating, the glue itself should run off the brush easily, and flat surfaces should be rubbed together to exclude all surplus glue, as well as to expell air bubbles. Joints should be cramped together as soon as possible after gluing, and it should be noted that a thick coating of glue will not make up for a slackly made joint. Glue can be waterproofed to a certain extent by adding about 10 per cent. of potassium bichromate solution.

A good liquid glue for ordinary use by melting Scotch glue with slightly less than the same weight of water in the manner described above. When cool, stir in 18 drams of glacial acetic acid to each pound of glue, and a tablespoonful of salicylate of soda. A semi-solid glue, requiring to be warmed before use, can be made by dissolving 4 ozs. of best Scotch glue in 16 ozs. of strong acetic acid. The advantage of ordinary liquid glue, or one of the patent tube glues, is that the adhesive can be applied cold. It sets quickly, but care should be exercised so that a very thin film of the glue is used. On no account should glue be applied to an old glued surface until it has been planed or scraped clean in order to expose the clean wood. This applies to greasy or dirty surfaces, for the utmost cleanliness should be observed, both as regards material and use.

ELECTRIC BELLS AND BATTERIES.

Faults in an electric bell system may be traced to various causes, but usually the cause of a failure to ring the bell when the push is pressed can be traced to a defective battery. It is possible that connections in the wiring have become loose or have corroded, and this sometimes happens to bell pushes exposed to rain or damp, but the first thing to do is to look at the battery.

Dry cells are now being fitted extensively to all modern bell circuits ; these, with the intermittent use that electric bells are normally subjected to, should last for a considerable period. In the event of a gradual weakness of the current, the addition of a new dry cell will generally effect an improvement.

Large numbers of the wet Leclanche cell are in common use, especially in old houses. These cells consist of an open glass jar, containing liquid, a central porous pot and a zinc rod. The liquid is made by dissolving sal ammoniac in water in the proportion of 2 ozs. of sal ammoniac to 1 pint of water, and it should be level with the black band marked on the outer bottle or jar.

In the course of time the water evaporates, and thus prevents the chemical action taking place. Usually a fresh supply of water will bring the battery up to full strength, but it is not a troublesome matter to mix up some new solution and fill up the battery again. Sal ammoniac can be purchased quite cheaply at most ironmongers and usually at all chemists. In examining the battery, it may be found that the liquid has crept up the connections and corroded them sufficiently to prevent close contact ; in this case the connections should be separated, scraped clean and fastened again.

In old batteries, the zinc rod may have been eaten away by the action of the chemical, but it is not a difficult matter to renew it. The porous pot is composed of a mixture of powdered carbon and oxide of manganese surrounding a central carbon rod ; it is very unusual for this portion of the battery to get out of order. The action of an old battery can be improved by coating the zinc rod with mercury ; this is termed amalgamating it, and is done by dipping the rod in a solution of sulphuric acid and rubbing it over with a little mercury applied with a piece of wash leather tied on to the end of a piece of wood.

Having tried the battery and remedied any fault found with it, and it is still impossible to get the bell to ring, it will be as well to unscrew the bell push and examine it. The action of the push is to make a contact, the two pieces of brass forming the inner connection should therefore be cleaned, and when pushed together form a close contact. If this does not cause the bell to ring the next point for examination is the bell itself.

To examine an electric bell, the cover should be removed and tested with an ordinary pocket lamp battery or any dry cell, if the terminals on the cell are attached to the terminals on the bell, the hammer should vibrate and ring the bell. If this does not happen, the contact between the screw on the pillar and the spring of the armature which touches the ends of the coils may be faulty, the point of the screw should be cleaned with a piece of fine emery cloth and readjusted.

There are other contact points connecting the wiring to the bell which should be examined, and if necessary, tightened up, and if the spring armature with its hammer extension works properly, the cell should be disconnected and the push tried again. If the bell does not work, it is possible that there may be a fault in the winding of the coils or their connections. The wire from the first cell terminal should pass through one coil to the next and on to the bracket supporting the spring armature. The wire from the other terminal should go direct to the pillar which carries the contact screw. The accuracy of all these contacts and circuits can be tested with a small pea bulb and a small cell.

Having tested the push, battery and bell, and still the battery does not fulfil its purpose, the fault must lie in the wiring somewhere, and the only way to find the fault is to examine the entire length of wiring. In many cases this is impossible, or at least difficult owing to the way the wiring is often hidden, but if it is taken in sections and each section tested with a small lamp and a cell, it will be possible to isolate the faulty section and deal with it. The method of testing is quite simple and consists in securing a lamp to one of the terminals of a small dry cell with a short length of insulated wire with bared ends. The other terminal of the cell has a similar length of wire attached. The two free ends of the wire should be attached to the wires which are normally attached to the battery or the bell whichever is nearer the push end of the circuit. The push should be pressed, and if that length of wiring is correct, the lamp will light. Take other sections in the same way and continue until the faulty section is discovered. New wiring should be installed when the fault is discovered, care being taken that it is properly insulated. In joining lengths of wire, it is always safer to solder the join.

REPAIRING BROKEN CHINA.

Broken china, earthenware and glass can be repaired in various ways depending upon the use to which the repaired article is to be put. If the broken article is of an ornamental character and is not subjected to much handling, the use of a cement or strong adhesive will generally suffice to hold the parts together ; but if the article is to be used and therefore liable to be washed frequently the broken parts should be rivetted together, and this method, when carefully done forms the most substantial way of effecting repairs.

The rivets are made from brass wire about $\frac{1}{16}$ in. in diameter, and are slightly flattened and bent in the form of a wide U about $\frac{1}{2}$ in. across, holes being drilled in the material, so that the ends of the rivet can be fixed in position. The main difficulty lies in the drilling of the china or earthenware, this is done with a V pointed highly tempered and hardened steel drill bit; the hole being about $\frac{1}{4}$ in. away from the broken edges. The lubricant generally used is turpentine.

It is sometimes difficult to pierce a very hard glazed surface, and in this case the usual practice is to use a diamond pointed drill, but as a general rule, if the point of the drill is quite sharp and has been thoroughly hardened, there are very few surfaces that will not yield to this treatment. In thin china it is usual to drill right through, but for thick earthenware, the depth need not be more than one half or two-thirds of the thickness. In all cases the hole must slope slightly inwards towards the break on both sides. Any form of small drill stock can be used, the cheap archimedian drill stock used by fretworkers is quite suitable; the important thing is the drill itself.

Having drilled the holes in pairs, opposite to one another, the next thing is to measure the distance between them, allow for the depth of the holes and then cut off the length of wire. The underside of the rivet is usually flattened so that it can lie flat on the material, the two ends being bent to the required slope and then the rivets are heated. The idea of heating them is to expand the metal so that when it cools and contracts, the broken parts will be drawn together tightly. Great care should be taken in fitting the rivets in position, they can be tapped in with a light wooden mallet if they do not fit in by the pressure of the fingers or a pair of pliers, but the nature of the material will not allow of any undue force being applied.

The final fixing of the rivet is done with either shellac or plaster of Paris, the former being applied hot and the latter cold, the cement will fill up the space surrounding the rivet and make it quite waterproof.

Glass can be drilled, but a good method of making a hole is to place a layer of stiff clay or putty over the part where the hole is desired and press down hard, make a small hole in the paste so as to uncover the exact place where the hole is to be, and then pour into this hole a little molten lead. Unless the glass is too thick, the piece of glass covered by the molten lead will immediately drop out, leaving a clean hole and the rest of the glass undamaged.

In repairing china by cement or adhesive, there are plenty of proprietary cements sold ready for use. The glues sold in tubes, of which there are several well known brands, are suitable for many purposes and in cases where the use of a glue is not advisable, plaster of Paris can be utilised. To make a really sound and lasting job, the repair should be done as soon as possible after the breakage occurs and while the fracture is quite clean. If this is impossible, the fractured edges must be thoroughly cleaned in hot water and dried before the application of the cement ; this applies particularly to surfaces that have been cemented before.

The fractured parts should be coated with the thinnest possible film of cement or glue and then they should be pressed together, not only to exclude the surplus adhesive, but also to prevent air bubbles forming inside the joint. Many people who use glue and other liquid adhesives make the mistake of coating the join with a thick layer, by doing this it is difficult to press the parts together and almost impossible to prevent fine air bubbles being left in the joint. In time these air bubbles expand and cause the joint to come undone. It is not always an easy matter to bind the cemented parts together, but it is very necessary that this should be done properly. When bound, the article should be placed on one side until the cement has had time to set.

In a bad fracture in china and crockery, it often happens that the edges of the broken parts are splintered, and in fitting the parts together, it may be found that some of the smaller particles are missing. The result is an open joint on the front or the back, and either the appearance of the front is marred or it is impossible to make a strong joint. With the aid of plaster of Paris, powdered whiting or even chalk, mixed with a little adhesive to form a paste, the space can be filled, smoothed down with a knife blade and when dry rubbed smooth with fine glasspaper. By adding a little fine powder colour to the paste, the colour of the object can be matched, and if it is necessary to apply a gloss, this can be done with transparent shellac varnish.

Plaster of Paris mixed with a strong solution of alum to the consistency of cream, is an excellent cement for all kinds of crockery, but it is more suitable for large surfaces than small. The white of egg is useful for delicate china ornaments. A good cement for china and other crockery is milk, the article should be bound up with the parts in position with string or tape, and then boiled in skimmed or ordinary milk. Broken glass can be joined with Canada balsam.

ELECTRIC LIGHT AND FUSES.

Exactly what to do when the electric light goes out is not quite clear to many boys and lack of the necessary knowledge may lead to considerable inconvenience, particularly if the failure of the light occurs in the evening or on Sunday when it is usually difficult to obtain the services of an electrician. If the filament of a lamp breaks, one light only is affected, but when all the lights go out, it may mean either a failure at the generating station or that the house circuit is broken.

It is probably understood that the ordinary filament lamp owes its capacity for giving light to the resistance to the current offered by the filament inside the lamp. The old form of carbon filament lamps are rarely used nowadays, those in ordinary use to-day are made with a metal filament and instead of the filament burning in a vacuum, the interior of the lamp is filled with nitrogen or some other gas, thus causing the filament to glow with a small amount of current.

If at any point in an electric lighting circuit, considerable resistance is offered to it, that portion of the wire becomes hot. The greater the resistance, the hotter the wire becomes, and in the case of an electric lamp, the resistance is so great and the conditions so favourable, that the wire glows with great brilliancy. If the wire forming the filament breaks, the current cannot flow and therefore the lamp will not light. If there were several lights on one circuit controlled by a switch, all the lamps would go out if one were to break, and to prevent this it is usual to connect up each light with a separate switch.

All electric lamps are constructed to suit a particular voltage, for example, lamps intended for a 100 volt installation would not be suitable for 200 volts. Care should be taken in fitting new lamps to see that they are made to suit the particular voltage of the supply. The wire used in conducting the current through the house is also dependent on the amount of the current, it would not do to use the wiring for an ordinary house with a maximum of ten lights for twice the number, nor would it do to carry out an extension for several lights with wire of a different diameter and resistance.

The method employed in electric wiring to prevent overheating which may be caused by an accidental overloading of current through, for example, the simultaneous burning of all the lamps in the circuit, is to include in the circuit one or more short lengths of easily fused wire. Thus if the current should at any time become more powerful than the wiring can stand, the fusible wire will melt and thus break the circuit and prevent the further flow of electricity. The length of wire is called a fuse, and it is contained in a porcelain framework or box, and in the case of the main fuses the porcelain fitting is placed inside a wooden or metal box with glass front, so that it can be readily inspected.

Where the cables enter the house, two sealed fuse boxes with glass fronts, one for each cable, will be found situated on the main supply side of the meter. These fuses must not be touched by the consumer, and if they happen to fail, the officials of the supply department should be notified. Next to the meter on the consumer's side, is the main double pole switch, this is composed of two tumbler switches connected by a wooden bar so that both work together. This switch when operated will cut off all current in the house.

After the switch comes a fuse box containing a pair of main fuses through which the whole of the house supply passes. Next comes a batch of three or more pairs of fuses, each pair carrying the current to a section of the house. Finally there may be a number of smaller fuses which are often far removed from the other fuses, and control the lighting of a single room.

When the light fails, the first thing to be done is to find which fuse has gone and then replace it. It is important to use the same kind of fuse wire as before, this can be obtained at most ironmongers or electrical dealers, it is made of an alloy, one part tin and two parts lead. Lead or tin wire will do for a temporary substitute, or a length of fine wire taken from a piece of ordinary flex, but on no account should ordinary bell wire be used. When effecting the renewal of a length of fuse wire, the current should be cut off at the main switch, but if the fault lies inside a room controlled by a small fuse and the fuse is inside the circuit controlled by the tumbler switch on the wall, the repair can be done providing the switch is out of action.

The operation of replacing a fuse is a simple matter as there is generally sufficient of the old wire left to act as a guide. A new length of fuse wire is laid in place with the ends wrapped round the terminal screws and is finally secured by screwing down the terminals but not tight enough to cut the wire. There are other forms of attaching the fuse wire in the box, among them being the cartridge, in this form the fuse wire is enclosed in a porcelain cylinder and is so made that the cartridge is pushed in position and screwed down. New cartridges containing wire are used to replace those that have been burnt out. As a temporary measure a length of fine wire can be wrapped round the cylinder before it is replaced, but a new cartridge should be fitted as soon as possible afterwards.

BOOK ENDS FROM SCRAP PIECES.

Book ends are always useful, and as they can be quickly and easily made from small pieces of wood they provide a good opportunity to make economical use of waste. The design shown at Fig. 1 illustrates a method of using three triangular pieces of floor board or similar material. Suitable pieces may be obtained most easily from the waste ends left by the carpenter or joiner. The direction of the grain need only be taken into consideration when the finished work is stained or varnished, and then it should be vertical or approximately so, as shown at Fig. 1. If in different directions, as shown at Fig. 2, it is better to finish the work with enamel paint or a cellulose paint.

The dimensions will depend on the material available, but with an equilateral shape, the sides should be from $4\frac{1}{2}$ in. to 7 in. long and the thickness from $\frac{3}{4}$ in. to 1 in. In all cases both surfaces and all edges should be made smooth with the plane. The middle one of the three pieces should be about $4\frac{1}{2}$ in., and the other two pieces say 1 in. larger and 1 in. smaller ; they need not be exactly 1 in., but both should be proportionate.

A piece of tinned sheet measuring $4\frac{1}{2}$ in. wide and at least the same length, preferably about 6 in., should be obtained so that it can be attached to the middle to form the base of the support. The tin, as shown at Fig. 3, should have perfectly smooth edges and be punched or drilled with three holes for attaching to the upright.

The largest piece should be grooved slightly to allow for the thickness of the tin base and the three pieces are then screwed and glued together after being thoroughly smoothed with glass paper. Care should be taken to drive the screws in when securing the metal plate, the sharp edges should be removed with a file so that there is no projection left that will be liable to scratch the table. The metal plate should, of course, be painted before being screwed on and the wood sized after staining and before varnishing. If cellulose paint is used it can be applied after the work is completed.

Another useful design is shown at Fig. 4. In this

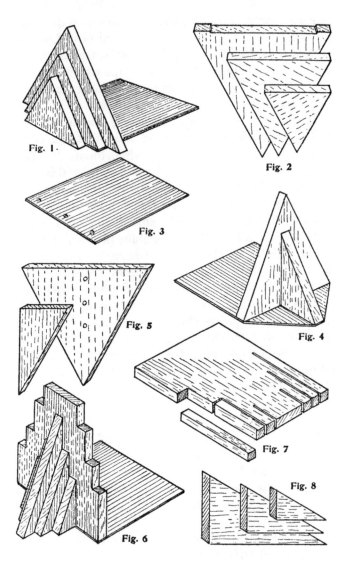

Fig. 1

Fig. 2

Fig. 3

Fig. 4

Fig. 5

Fig. 6

Fig. 7

Fig. 8

case the large triangle should be about 6 in. wide and at least 9 in. long. The two pieces of wood, as shown at Fig. 5, should be screwed together, the smaller piece being of the same shape as a 60 degree set square. The outer corners should be trimmed off to the shape shown.

An effective yet simple design is shown at Fig. 6 ; this uses a little more wood and takes longer to make, but it looks very well when finished. The main upright, measuring about $7\frac{1}{2}$ in. by 6 in., as shown at Fig. 7, is prepared by making three saw cuts each side to form the steps. The sawn surfaces should be made quite smooth, using a chisel or, if desired, a file. The triangular pieces should be stepped down in the same proportion as the sides, that so the top of the outer pieces are on a level with the first notch, the second pieces with the second notch and the centre piece with the third notch. These pieces should be glued together and then screwed to the uprights. It is advisable to make the metal plate long enough to cover the triangular pieces as in Fig. 4, and trim the ends close to the wood.

A TEA TRAY.

By using plywood, the making of trays is not a difficult job and with a little care an attractive tea tray can be made for a few pence. In the design shown at Fig. 1 the base is made from $\frac{3}{16}$ in. thick Oregon pine plywood, with a border of 1 in. by $\frac{3}{4}$ in. clean yellow deal or whitewood. The corners are made with the sawn mitre joint and covered with pewter.

Begin by making quite sure that the plywood for the bottom of the tray has square corners and parallel sides. The sides and ends are measured and suitable lengths of 1 in. by $\frac{3}{4}$ in. or $\frac{5}{8}$ in. are cut off. The ends are cut off to an angle of 45 degrees and are fitted on the base. The edges are now screwed on from underneath and then the corner plates prepared as shown at Fig. 2. The pewter pieces should be from $3\frac{1}{2}$ in. to 4 in. long and wide enough to cover the outside, top and inside as indicated. The material can be obtained in several thicknesses, anything from Nos. 20 to 24 S.W.G. will do, although it can be thicker. The four corner pieces should be cut to the shape shown, and to avoid mistakes it is better to cut out a shape in stiff paper and fit it in position. The shapes when completed should be fastened on with screws and nails after finishing the wood with stain or paint.

An effective method with either of the above methods of finishing is to stencil a pattern at each corner, using a stencil plate as shown at Fig. 3.

A pleasing method of treating the corners of the tray edges is shown at Fig. 4. The cuts are easily made with a sharp knife and if the spaces are accurately marked out and carefully cut the result is very effective. It is preferable to use hardwood if the decorative cuts shown at Fig. 4 are to be used. Oak in this case will be found quite satisfactory, and it is possible to obtain plywood faced with oak at very little extra cost. The difference in strength and appearance when using oak makes its use well worth while.

A DOG KENNEL.

A dog kennel is quite a simple job to make and the design given at Fig. 1, although it has definite dimensions, can be altered to suit a larger dog. It has a distinct advantage over the ordinary dog kennel, apart from the platform in front, in so much that the upper portion can be taken off, leaving a perfectly even floor. This allows of the thorough cleansing of the interior, a somewhat difficult job in a small kennel.

There are eight distinct parts used in the construction, the floor, the two sides with a connecting piece, the front, back and two portions of the roof. Ordinary yellow deal tongued and grooved board about $\frac{3}{4}$ in. thick should be used. The boarding may be that known as match boarding, but short lengths of tongued and grooved floor boards will be found quite satisfactory and can be obtained usually without difficulty.

Begin by making the two side pieces as at Fig. 2. The centre board should be cut to a length of $17\frac{1}{2}$ in. and the outer pieces to 16 in., leaving a trifle on the length so that the ends can be planed smooth. If the material is 9 in. wide, the outside boards should be cut down equally so as to give a total width of 24 in. when the three pieces are drawn up close. The two cross pieces should be 2 in. by 1 in., and are $20\frac{1}{2}$ in. long; this provides for sufficient at the ends to allow for the end pieces. The middle projecting piece should be trimmed off to about 8 in. wide. The cross pieces can be nailed, but screwing is much stronger.

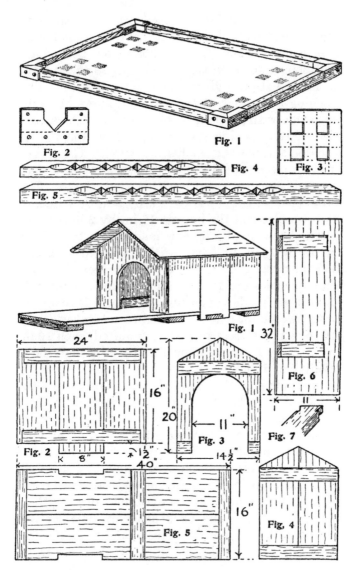

Fig. 1

Fig. 2

Fig. 4

Fig. 5

Fig. 3

Fig. 1

24″

16″

20″

11″

Fig. 2

Fig. 3

8″

12″

40″

14½″

16″

Fig. 5

32″

Fig. 6

11″

Fig. 7

Fig. 4

The front and back pieces are both alike as regards width and height, but the front, as at Fig. 3, is of course open. The two boards are 20 in. long and planed down on the outer edges, so that a total width of $14\frac{1}{2}$ in. is given when close together. The opening is circular at the top and allows of $1\frac{3}{4}$ in. each side with a height of 14 in. or so. The actual size of the opening should depend on the size of the dog and may be smaller if desired. The curves in each piece should be cut with a bow saw or pad saw and finished smooth with a spokeshave. The cross piece at the top is $14\frac{1}{2}$ in. by 2 in by 1 in. and the two pieces at the bottom $1\frac{3}{4}$ in. by 2 in by 1 in.

The back, as at Fig. 4, is made from two pieces 20 in. by $7\frac{1}{4}$ in. by $\frac{3}{4}$ in., with two cross pieces, $14\frac{1}{2}$ in. by 2 in. by 1 in. It will be seen that the outside edges are 16 in. high after the sloping cuts have been made. The floor at Fig. 5 is made up with two 40 in. lengths planed to a total width of 16 in. Three cross pieces are required, each 16 in. by 2 in. by 1 in. ; if some 2 in. by 2 in. material is available, it should be used.

The side pieces are now placed in position on the floor so that the slots can be marked out. They are sawn and chiselled out and then the cross piece to join them, measuring 16 in. by 2 in. by 1 in., should be prepared. It will be seen at Fig. 7 that the ends of this cross piece are sawn to a dovetail. The strips placed in position and marked on the middle pieces and the grooves cut to a depth of 1 in. The front and back piece are now screwed on or nailed to the side pieces, and then the two portions of the roof, as shown at Fig. 6, can be prepared. It is an advantage to use two 32 in. lengths of 11 in. board $\frac{3}{4}$ in. thick. The two cross pieces are 2 in. by 1 in. and should be marked off and cut to the length of the slope at the ends. The pieces fit inside so as to leave a projection of 2 in. at the back ; thus the distance from the back should be $2\frac{3}{4}$ in. and from the outside edges the length is $20\frac{1}{2}$ in.

The boards are bevelled on the inside or meeting edges and are then screwed in position. The top may be covered with roofing felt if desired, but if all the outside wood is thoroughly well coated with paint this will not be essential. The connecting bar under the floor is screwed in place after painting and after the inside of the kennel has been coated with lime wash. This completes the work.

INDEX

THE LONDON AND NORWICH PRESS, LIMITED, ST. GILES' WORKS, NORWICH

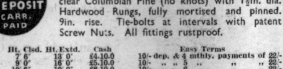